The 2024

# Guide to Colorado Real Estate Investing Strategies

Published by:

Chris Lopez

2755 South Locust St #150

Denver, CO 80222

www.DenverInvestmentRealEstate.com

# Dedication

For Steven Posusta, a valued teammate whose passion and dedication inspired us all. You are deeply missed.

# Contents

# Thank You

This book continues to be one of my favorite projects each year and wouldn't be possible without our contributors.  I sincerely appreciate people continuing to share their journey and be brave enough to publish their goals with this community.  With the market last year, it's been fun reading how people are pivoting or staying steady but ultimately continuing to invest in real estate in creative ways which motivates me and generates new ideas. Thank you for contributing!

| | | |
|---|---|---|
| Eric Garber | Mitch Conrad | Miller McSwain |
| Nick Elder | Jeffrey White | Joey Schneider |
| Laura Pilcher | Jeff Giesen | Ken Hobbick |
| James Brown | Jim Tiernan | Toby Hanson |
| Benjamin Einspahr | Jamin Cook | Chris Lawhead |
| Jake Cohen | Jared Carlson | Heidi Jensen |
| Shawn Riley | Matt Amundson | Vikas Agarwal |
| Brandon Scholten | Kelly Mahana | Phillip Austin |
| Stephen Lepke | Paul DeSalvo | Caitlin Logue |

# Do Your Due Diligence

Some of this book's contributors are my clients. I asked them to contribute because their strategies can help others. Also, it forces them to clarify their goals in writing which allows me to do a better job of executing their strategies with them. Other contributors are real estate professionals who have services or potential deals for investors. This book is not an endorsement of any of the contributors' strategies, services, or potential deals.

Do your own due diligence!

# Introduction

Each year I publish a new edition of the **Colorado Real Estate Investing Guide**. I'm proud this 6<sup>th</sup> edition is in your hands! The book is about Colorado investors sharing their real estate investing strategies and goals. The goal of the book is to share ideas and connect people around town to grow your knowledge and your network.

This books' crowd-sourced chapters are a goldmine of information and investment ideas. After reading all the chapters, I have detailed notes for people I want to connect with and strategies that I want to explore for my own investing. Hopefully you walk away with knowledge and action items too.

Many of our chapters are from returning contributors. I love seeing the evolution of the investor's strategies and mindset. Mine changes every year. As a reminder, change is the only constant. No plan is perfect or goes unchanged.

In previous editions, I wrote detailed investing guides for Denver and Colorado Springs. It seemed like a great idea; people could get a copy, read one chapter, and have a solid understanding of the market. The data grows stale too fast for a book. Instead, visit www.DenverInvestmentRealEstate.com for current trends and deal analyses.

I'm very appreciative of chapters from new contributors, who are often newer investors. It's a lot to put yourself and your goals out there publicly.

Enjoy the 2024 edition!

Chris Lopez

P.S. If you have any questions from this book or want to talk investing strategies, please reach out to me at Chris@envisionrea.com.

## Start Your Real Estate Investing Plan Today!

### Schedule Your Free Consultation Today To Learn:

- One on One Guidance: We want to get to know you, your long term goals, and investing situation.

- An Investing Strategy Tailored to You: Because every investor's lifestyle and goals are different.

- A Clear Action Plan: You'll walk away knowing exactly what steps you need to take to start your investing journey.

# 2024 Annual Investing Newsletter

Dear Fellow Investors,

The new high-interest rate market cycle changed the investing landscape. This annual letter outlines the key market trends and opportunities and explains how to position your real estate portfolio accordingly.

After studying the trends and identifying the opportunities, I made significant changes to my investing strategy and rental portfolio. Hopefully, understanding these trends helps you pivot and thrive in the current market.

Understanding current real estate market trends in Colorado is crucial for investing success. The Denver, Colorado Springs, Pueblo, and Northern Colorado markets follow similar patterns, so I'll speak to the overall trends. Our quarterly market trend packets and monthly podcasts provide more granular details if you need them at www.DenverInvestmentRealEstate.com

Interest rates have shot up and remain high, making it very challenging to achieve positive cash flow. However, there are still opportunities if you're creative and willing to put in some sweat equity.

## Strong Headwinds

After the 2008 crash and recovery, Colorado real estate had solid tailwinds for many years. But not anymore. 2024 will see these continued headwinds:

- High interest rates, with home prices staying relatively high.

- Below average home price appreciation, likely 1-4%.

- Below average rent growth.

- Big increases in property taxes.

- Significant increases in insurance costs.

- Landlord unfriendly legislation that passed in 2023, with more potentially coming in 2024.

It's doubtful that we'll see prices drop, let alone a crash. Rather, the easy days of double-digit investment returns are over. Colorado's price and rent appreciation exceeded the historical averages for the last ten years. Averages are made over the long run. I expect price and rent growth will be below the historical averages for the next 3-7 years.

## Deal Landscape and Opportunities

- Long-term rentals with property management: Requiring down payments of 30-40%, these investments offer the prospect of low cash-on-cash returns across single-family homes to fourplexes.

- Short-term rentals: This segment has experienced a contraction in revenue and demand, prompting some investors to withdraw from the market. Fewer newcomers are venturing into short-term rentals due to the prevailing economics and the increasing hostility from municipalities.

- Medium-term rentals (30+ days): This niche has flourished recently, catering to traveling nurses, digital nomads, and those in transition. However, reports of softening demand and an influx of short-term rentals pivoting to this model are making it harder to find great deals. They are out there; just double-check your numbers and location.

- Room-by-room rentals: Individually renting rooms generates the most substantial cash flow in the market cycle. Many Denver-area homes present the potential for adding bedrooms, often in the basement, with minimal expense. Some investors have capitalized on this trend by curating theme-oriented rentals and fostering communities aligned with specific interests, such as women entrepreneurs or coders, yielding remarkable results.

- New construction investments: With new build and resale prices often on par, investing in newly built townhomes or single-family homes has emerged as a viable strategy for those seeking to park capital with minimal property maintenance burdens. These investments can be viewed as secure holdings in prime locations, akin to bonds. Expect a 30-40% down payment.

## Fact: It's tough to find cash flowing rentals in today's market.

Other notable trends:

- DSCR and other long term investor loans sometimes have better rates than a 30-year conventional. If you're looking to put long term debt on a property, definitely explore your options and various lending products.

- Section 8 rentals are in high demand. There are more people with vouchers than properties available, and many landlords are receiving market rent or sometimes a premium.

- With the 2023 and 2024 proposed legislation, managing your properties is becoming more challenging for self-managing landlords. If you self-manage, review the legislation and update your leases and processes accordingly.

In summary, generating strong returns is difficult now for hands-off landlords; however, active landlords can still find viable opportunities through strategies like house hacking, medium-term rentals, and room-by-room rentals.

**Let's answer two of the most common questions:**

1. "Chris, if I'm a newer / less money / more time investor, what do you recommend?"

   a. If I were new and starting over today, I'd house hack to build a room-by-room rental portfolio. If I couldn't house hack, I would focus on room-by-room rentals.

2. "Chris, If I have more money / less time / hands-off investor, what do you recommend?"

   a. The current rental returns are not very attractive. I'm investing passively to take advantage of the commercial estate reckoning (more below). If I were to buy any directly owned rentals, I'd buy new-build single-family homes with a 4-7 year exit plan to recycle the capital.

3. "Chris, what moves do I make in my portfolio when traditional rentals don't make sense?"

   a. This is probably the most common question I'm asked, and it's obvious why: The investing strategies investors are using no longer work in this new, high-rate market cycle.

The two common ones:

**Cash-out refinance to buy another rental**: It no longer makes sense as it turns the current property into negative cash flow.

**Sell and trade up with a 1031 exchange:** With the higher down payments, it often becomes a lateral or marginal trade-up. In my investing chapter, I have a detailed example of selling a condo and potentially 1031ing into a fourplex. The numbers didn't work!

We cannot change the market, so we must change with the market.

## Where's the Next Opportunity?

The spike in interest rates is causing havoc for commercial real estate because they don't have 30-year fixed interest rates. The rates are usually locked for 1-7 years before resetting or floating to current rates, often double their initial rate! Once you add on higher insurance and taxes, the deals usually don't pencil out. This creates distress... and opportunity!

Commercial real estate is a broad term that includes industrial, retail, office, apartments (anything with 5+ units is commercial real estate), ground-up development projects, self-storage, student housing, and build-to-rent projects—basically, anything that is not a 1–4 unit residential property.

This Wall Street Journal article from August 15, 2023, sums up the opportunity: "Wall Street Is Ready to Scoop Up Commercial Real Estate on the Cheap. Firms are raising billions of dollars for funds to target assets with slumping values".

**34 Unit Apartment Deal Example**

The best way to explain the opportunity is to walk through a deal I'm a general partner in. In November 2022, we purchased an off-market 34-unit apartment building in north Denver. Due to the market slowdown, we negotiated an attractive price (around 2019 prices!). The property is outdated, and there is significant room (40-60%) to raise rents to market.

Here's the property overview:

- The project is made up of two 17-unit buildings that need renovation. There is significant room (40-60%) to raise rents to market.

- 15 minutes to downtown Denver and close to light rail.

- 32x 1-bedroom and 2x 2-bedroom units.

- 1970's vintage; very few modern updates currently.

Here's the value-add business plan:

- Renovate exterior.

- Improve all interior units.

- $930,000 capital improvement budget.

- The business plan is very familiar to the Sponsor.

- Raise rents from current ($815) to $1300-1400 (market).

Property Numbers:

- Purchase price: $5,350,000

- Acquisition/closing cost: $99,875

- Working capital: $216,486

- Capex budget: $933,639

- Total: $6,600,000

Financing:

- Equity $2,200,000

- Financing: $4,400,000

- Rate is 5.9%, 18 months of interest only (IO) payments, 30-year amortization

After the property is renovated and stabilized, we're aiming to sell it for around $7,800,000. To summarize, we're buying this property at a great price to rehab it, raise rents, and then sell it. This is the equivalent of an apartment building flip over two to three years.

As 2023 wraps up, I'm happy to share that the project is on track. All the units are renovated and are at the estimated market rent forecast. The investors will have their first cash flow distribution in Q1. We're looking to sell it in 2024.

## How to Invest in Commercial Deals?

The numbers of the 34-unit apartment building deal probably excite you, but you are also wondering how to access these deals. As an investor, I went through a paradigm and strategy shift. I can't source and run these deals like I did with my residential investments in the previous market cycle.

The deals are bigger and more complex. As an individual, I didn't have the operations or the $2.2 million required to execute this deal on my own. Passive investing is the broad term that enables participation in these types of transactions. Passive real estate investing refers to investment strategies where the investor is not actively involved in the day-to-day management or operations of the real estate property. In other words, the investor takes a hands-off approach and relies on others to manage the property.

The advantages of real estate syndications (a form of passive investing) include access to more extensive, institutional-grade properties, professional management, and the potential for higher returns compared to smaller individual investments. However, they also come with risks, such as illiquidity (the inability to sell your investment easily) and the possibility of losing your entire investment if the property underperforms.

## Is Syndication a Dirty Word Now?

During the market's upswing, many investors embraced syndications. However, as the market shifts and some deals falter, I've noticed a change in sentiment. The word "syndication" often carries a negative connotation, akin to profanity. Some syndicators who raised funds to acquire properties before interest rates spiked are now pausing distributions, calling for additional capital to sustain investments, or selling properties, resulting in complete losses for their investors. Disastrous news for those investors!

While some individuals are losing money and some syndicators are going out of business, it doesn't mean all syndications are inherently flawed. If you get food poisoning, do you swear off eating altogether? Of course not. But you'd certainly avoid the restaurant that made you ill.

It's crucial to thoroughly review the offering memorandum, understand the risks involved, and conduct due diligence on the Sponsor's track record and the specific investment opportunity before investing in a real estate syndication.

## Capitalizing on Market Cycles: Selling High, Buying Low

The age-old investing adage "buy low, sell high" is widely known. However, the challenge often lies in identifying where to reinvest to truly "buy low." The current market cycle presents an exceptional opportunity to "sell high" with our residential properties and subsequently "buy low" with distressed commercial assets, such as the 34-unit apartment building example.

I've been anticipating the next significant real estate market opportunity for years. I firmly believe this is the most advantageous opportunity since the 2008 real estate crash to acquire properties at discounted prices. Consequently, I am selling most of my residential rental portfolio to reinvest passively in these undervalued commercial opportunities.

This quote resonates deeply with me: "History doesn't repeat itself, but it often rhymes." – Mark Twain.

I vowed that when the next 2008-like situation presented itself, I would pivot to take advantage, and that's precisely what I'm doing now. My personal investing strategy chapter goes into specific details and moves I'm making in my portfolio.

## Optimizing Your Portfolio: Aligning Investments with Goals

Many investors are excited about the current market conditions but are unsure of the best strategies to optimize their portfolios. Before making any portfolio changes, I strongly recommend reviewing your current performance and revisiting your goals. The most effective moves align with your risk tolerance and investment objectives.

This is precisely why we created the Property Llama online app – to help investors understand how their current portfolio performs. Investors often fall into the trap of reminiscing about "that amazing property I bought 9 years ago..." Don't get stuck in the past! How is that asset performing today?

If you need assistance, visit PropertyLlama.com and follow these four steps:

1. Upload Your Properties and Define Your Goals.

2. Benchmark and Track Asset Performance.

3. Model Different "What If" Scenarios.

4. Uncover Hidden Opportunities to Accelerate Returns.

By aligning your portfolio with your current goals and risk tolerance, you can make informed decisions and optimize your investments for long-term success.

## What's Your Goal: Income or Growth?

One of the first questions I ask investors is, "Are you in growth mode or income mode?" Many investors have not clearly identified their mode, which often creates friction when managing their portfolios.

Growth investing and income investing are two different approaches, each with its own objectives and strategies. Here's an explanation of the two:

**Growth Investing:**

Growth investing is a strategy focused on capital appreciation. Investors aim to purchase assets that have the potential for significant growth in value over time. The primary goal is to achieve substantial gains by investing in assets experiencing rapid growth or potential for future growth.

Key characteristics of growth investing:

- Focus on capital appreciation rather than current income.

- Investing in assets with high growth potential.

- Willing to accept higher risk for potentially higher returns.

- Longer investment horizons.

- Emphasis on future earnings and revenue growth.

**Income Investing:**

On the other hand, income investing is a strategy that prioritizes generating a steady stream of income from investments. Investors who follow this approach seek assets that provide regular cash flows, such as stock dividends or interest from bonds. The primary goal is to generate a consistent income stream rather than capital appreciation.

Key characteristics of income investing:

- Focus on generating regular income payments.

- Investing in assets with stable and predictable cash flows.

- Lower risk tolerance, as preservation of capital is important.

- Shorter investment horizons, as income is the priority.

- Emphasis on current yield and income generation.

It's important to note that these two approaches are not mutually exclusive. Investors may choose to combine elements of growth and income investing to create a diversified portfolio that aligns with their specific goals, risk tolerance, and investment horizon.

Growth investing tends to be more suitable for investors with a longer time horizon and a higher risk tolerance, as the potential for capital appreciation often comes with higher volatility. Income investing, on the other hand, may be more appropriate for investors seeking a steady stream of income, such as retirees or those with a lower risk tolerance.

Ultimately, the choice between growth investing and income investing depends on an investor's personal financial goals, risk profile, and investment time frame.

Are you primarily focused on growth or income?

I'm currently growth oriented.

# Passive Opportunities for Income: Be the Bank

High Interest rates have made it hard to find cash-flowing rentals, but they also make it a great time to "be the bank." Debt Funds can be a great way to achieve cash flow in today's market.

I've always been intrigued with investors who have lent money to other investors. However, I don't have the time or desire to look for investors and underwrite their deals. Plus, I've heard a few horror stories of investors having to foreclose on a property in another state. The industry norm is a 2-3% foreclosure rate with loans like this. Usually, foreclosures are still profitable, but you must deal with the foreclosure process. They will happen; I just don't want to deal with it.

I started investing in debt funds a few years ago and have loved it. They provided the diversification and passive role that I was seeking. If you're looking for cash flow, explore the world of debt funds.

**What is a debt fund?** A private lending debt fund fills the need in the market for loans that are not standard agency loans (for example, 30-year fixed on your primary) and bank loans. Debt funds take money from private investors (for example, you) and lend the money out to individual borrowers.

## How Debt Funds Offer Superior Diversification Compared to Individual Notes

A debt fund operates by writing loans and collecting the principal, interest, and associated fees. The fund then passes the collected funds to its investors through quarterly interest payments. Investing in a debt fund allows investors to spread their risk across dozens of properties at once, with professionals managing the underwriting, loan draws, and servicing.

When investors attempt to manage loans themselves, they concentrate their risk on a single property, which can be problematic if the property is located out of state. If things go wrong, the investor may be forced to foreclose on the property, which can be risky and time-consuming.

The fund approach offers diversification by spreading investments across multiple assets, typically dozens of properties, and numerous borrowers in various markets. The fund guarantees investors' investments in the fund, while the fund's loans are secured by the borrowers' mortgages, properties, and other assets.

**What type of returns can you expect?**

- Annual returns in the 8-12% range.

- Most funds have a one to two year lock-up period; then, your investment is liquid.

- Most funds pay quarterly distributions or allow you to reinvest for compounding.

- Minimum investment range is typically $10,000 - $100,000.

# Passive Opportunities for Growth Investing

Here are the trends and opportunities that I'm following:

Value-Add Multifamily:

- Identify underperforming multifamily properties in desirable areas.

- Implement capital improvements and renovations to units and common areas.

- Raise rents to market rates after renovations, increasing property value.

- Potential for forced appreciation through strategic value-add plays.

Build-to-Rent Development:

- Capitalize on the growing demand for single-family rental homes.

- Develop new communities of rental homes in high-growth markets.

- Benefit from economies of scale in construction and property management.

- Potential for long-term rental income and asset appreciation.

Self-Storage:

- Relatively recession-resistant asset class with consistent demand.

- Opportunities in expanding markets or underserved areas.

- Implement technology and automation to improve operations.

- Potential for value-add plays by acquiring and renovating older facilities.

Build-to-Sell Residential Development:

- Identify markets with strong housing demand and limited supply.

- Acquire land and construct new single-family or multifamily communities.

- Focus on efficient construction processes and desirable amenities.

- Potential for significant returns by delivering in-demand housing products.

Office Conversion to Apartments:

- With the office sector crashing, I explored conversion opportunities.

- While it sounds good in theory, only about 5-10% of office buildings could be converted.

- For most, it's just not economically feasible. You're better off demolishing the office building to build a new apartment.

Long-Term Stay Hotels:

- Tap into the growing demand for extended-stay accommodations for economy focused long-term stay hotels.

- Acquire and renovate existing hotels or develop new purpose-built facilities.

- Cater to corporate travelers, relocations, and long-term projects.

- Potential for stable income streams and value-add opportunities.

## Portfolio Rebalancing Considerations

Given the insights shared, I encourage you to evaluate your current portfolio allocation and consider moving to align your portfolio with your goals. I invite you to create a free account at www.PropertyLlama.com to help optimize your portfolio.

The words of wisdom from legendary investor Warren Buffett, " Be fearful when others are greedy, and greedy when others are fearful," ring particularly true in the current market climate. While the prevailing conditions present challenges, they also unveil attractive prospects for investors.

Regardless of the portfolio adjustments you elect to pursue, it is imperative to conduct rigorous market research, thorough due diligence, and a comprehensive risk assessment for any potential real estate investment.


Yours sincerely,

Chris Lopez

## Denver Real Estate Investing Podcast - Denver Investing Market News

### Subscribe To Get New Episodes Every Week

Gain important information about a different segment of the Denver market every week. Join host Chris Lopez as he covers everything from the basics of real estate investing to current market trends. Learn how to analyze real estate deals and listen to interviews with local experts and investors at every step of the investing journey.

## Property Llama: Crystal-Clear Insights for Bold Investment Moves

### Start Analyzing Your Properties & Building Wealth Today

- Property Llama simplifies the process of optimizing your real estate.

- Dive deep into property equity analysis. identify underperforming assets, reposition them into higher-performing rentals, and accelerate your wealth building.

- Investor accounts are free for life!

# Investors' Strategies

As always, we invite all investors to contribute a chapter to this book. The one requirement is a Colorado connection. That can mean that you live and invest in Colorado, that you live in Colorado and invest out of state, or that you live out of state but invest in Colorado.

If you are just starting on your investing journey, I encourage you to contribute as well. It is a great way to clarify your strategy and put your goals to paper. Hold yourself accountable and start networking.

I hope everyone can use this book as a networking tool and connect with other investors as mentors, sounding boards, and collaborators to help each other and achieve those investing goals.

The submission details and dates for the 2025 book are at www.denverinvestmentrealestate.com/contribute

I hope you enjoy reading everyone's strategies as much as I do.

# Benjamin R. Einspahr

Pivot, Pivot, PIVOT!!! Insert GIF from Friends where Ross is trying to move a couch up the stairs. Pivot was the theme of my 2023 and new 2024 goals. From career change to relocating to Parker and baby number 2 on the way, it has been a journey.

I have been investing in real estate since 2017 and contributing to the Colorado Real Estate Investing Strategies Book since 2020. It is safe to say that every year, my goals (both short-term and long-term) change as my life changes. I say this to stress the importance of:

5. Writing down your goals.

6. Reviewing them annually.

7. Understand that your goals will change as the years go by.

## About Me

I live in Parker, CO (as of 12/28/23) with my lovely wife Alyson, daughter Emma, and our newest addition coming in the Spring of 2024. Wooohoooo!!! I work in the Commercial Construction Industry for JD Steel and am actively studying to get my real estate license. My wife and I self-manage all our rental properties in Denver, consisting of 2 LTRs and 3 MTRs. Well, as I am writing this, 2 MTRs, but by the time the book has been published, we will finish turning our basement into a separate mother-in-law income suite and rent it out as an MTR—more details in my 2024 goals below.

We also have a rental property in Omaha, NE. It is finally under property management. It only took 5 years of self-management from out of state! Never again.

In addition, I host a monthly real estate meetup with Jeff White (the poster child of house hacking) and Troy Howell with Nova Home Loans. This monthly meetup is tailored to anyone who is an active house hacker, interested in house hacking, or just looking to expand their network with like-minded individuals.

Scan here to get the details of our next meetup:

## About My Strategy:

My strategy is not flashy. Some may say that it is boring, but boring is good when it comes to REI. Here is what I do and have done since 2017: I buy a single-family home with a 5% down loan and rent out a portion of the house while living there to offset my living expenses.

After 12-24 months have gone by, move out and turn the home into a rental property. Then rinse and repeat. I have done this 4 times over the past 7 years. Shout out to Local N Long Distance Movers. They were terrific to work with.

This slow yet steady strategy has allowed me the flexibility to escape a career I was not too thrilled about, help other savvy investors execute the same strategy I mentioned above, AND, most importantly, allow my wife the flexibility to stay at home and raise our beautiful family.

## 2023 Goal Review and Results

Personal Goal: Read 1 Book Per Quarter

I have had this goal for the past four years now. The 4 books I read:

1. Make Your Bed by William H McRaven

2. Pitch Anything by Oren Klaff

3. No Excuses by Bryan Tracy.

    a. This is an old-school audiobook. You can hear the author turn the pages as he reads it!

4. What If God Wrote Your To-Do List by Jay Payleitner

5. BONUS BOOK: Smart Brevity by Jim VandeHei

Fitness Goal: Running a 10k (6.2 miles) race within 48 minutes.

I did not hit this goal. I tried it twice and missed it by about 20 seconds each time. I needed to put in the proper training required to execute: less strength training and more running.

## RE and Financial Goal #1: Financing for HH#4

This goal put me in a solid financial position to purchase the next house hack. This needed to be done through savings growth, identifying capital for the acquisition of the property, and, most importantly, the ability to be lending qualified.

With the changes in the RE Market and the difficulty of getting pre-approved with 1099, I made the difficult decision to return to the commercial world. The transition has turned out much better than expected and ended up being an excellent win-win for all!

Quick Tip: Lenders LOVE people with stable W2 income. 1099/ self-employed, not so much.

## RE and Financial Goal #2: Acquisition of HH#4

Closed on HH#4 on 12/28/23! This is more of a lifestyle house hack. We are still renting out a small portion of the home but did not purchase it with the intention of turning it into a future rental. In fact, if you look at it from a number's perspective, numbers don't pan out. But numbers are not everything. This is a home we will be able to nest in for the next 5+ years and raise our family. My wife says 18+ years :)

RE and Financial Goal #3: Sell Omaha Rental

I originally planned to sell my rental property in Omaha in 2023 and do a 1031 exchange for a rental property in Colorado Springs or Pueblo. I did not end up selling. Instead, I kept it and put it under property management to give me back my time and let the professionals do what they do best.

# 2024 Goals

### Real Estate Goal #1: Renovation of the basement to Mother-In-Law (MIL) Suite

I will use the HELOC taken out on our Wheat Ridge Townhome Rental to renovate the basement in our current home in Parker and turn it into a small income suite. The 1 bed/1 bath, 500 SF rental will have a bedroom, living space, mini kitchenette, and full bathroom: no washer and dryer.

Conservatively estimating $50/sf and $5000 for furnishings. Estimating between $1,600 -$1,800 per month income.

### Real Estate Goal #2: Complete My RE License

Working with Chris Lopez and the Envision Advisors Team has been a fantastic experience, and it has been very much like drinking real estate investing through a firehose... to say the least. I am going to leverage the education I have learned over the past five years to help others achieve their goals through real estate investing. This will be done as a side hobby while still working my W2 at JD Steel.

I started studying for the exam in Q4 of 2023 but put it on the back burner when transitioning to JD Steel and acquiring HH #4. My goal is to complete it by mid-2024.

### Investing Goal #1: Sell Omaha Rental and Diversify Assets

The lease on my Omaha Rental is up in September of 2024. After that lease is up, I will sell the rental and leverage the proceeds in 3 different ways:

1. Pay off most of my HELOC used to fund the down payment of my current HH and renovate the basement MIL. I say "most" because there is a penalty for paying off the HELOC in 3 years or less. After 3 years, I'll pay it off 100%!

2. Invest in some low-index funds/ ITFs.

3. Build up my savings to be more cash heavy.

### Personal Goal #1: Exercise Routine Transition PM -> AM

For years, I have exercised in the evenings after work. It is more challenging to do that now with longer working hours and wanting to spend as much time as possible with my family on weekdays.

In 2024, that will transition to morning workouts before work. It takes more planning when I must be at work by 6:30

AM. A few things I will change to ensure success and consistency are utilizing the gym showers and kitchenette at work so I can easily prep breakfast and lunch.

Thank you for reading my chapter. If you would like to connect with me, please don't hesitate to reach out.

Email: Ben@HouseHackStack.com

# Brandon Scholten

Brandon Scholten is a buy-and-hold real estate investor and the owner of Keyrenter Property Management Denver, which manages rental properties for investors in the Denver metro area. He is the co-host of the Denver Landlord's Podcast.

Connect with Brandon at (720)-735-7497, brandon@keyrenterdenver.com, or www.keyrenterdenver.com.

## About My Strategy

I bought my first rental property, a run-down 1-bedroom condo, with two partners in 2012. I then held onto the condo I had been living in when I bought a new primary the following year. I purchased three more condos with those partners and held on to another primary when I moved again. Along the way, I did end up selling my first condo when I could still take the gains tax-free (See IRS publication 523) and upgraded our primary residence again to accommodate our growing family (my wife and I now have three kids - ages 9, 7, and 3). 2015, I started a property management company called Keyrenter Property Management Denver. As years passed and this business was growing, I found that it used up a lot of my available cash, and as rental property prices have increased, my portfolio's growth has stalled. The last rental property I bought was a duplex in Littleton in 2018, for which I utilized the BRRR strategy (minus the repeat part of the equation). I did a major renovation on the property, adding a bedroom to one side and a bedroom and bathroom to the other.

One of the tensions I've faced is that growing the property management company has required me to divert time, money, and energy away from developing my real estate portfolio. The property management company generates both personal income and a growing asset value, such that the value of the business is worth several million dollars today. I don't have any plans to sell the company, but I believe it's important, like buying and holding real estate, to be aware of the asset value growth, equity position, and cash flow. My personal income has not grown relative to the business revenue growth in the last couple of years, and you'll see that reflected in the first goal for 2023 that I discuss below.

I'm part of a peer advisory group of CEOs through an organization called Convene. Each year, we do a yearly goal-setting practice, which plays a significant role in the goals I develop each year. This process starts with a life analytics tool that helps identify areas where I'm struggling or want to improve. The tool allows me to rate myself on a series of statements, like "you regularly learn something new or read a book that improves your organizational performance." This example falls under the professional growth category. Once I rate myself on all the statements, a chart shows how I am doing in different areas of life. From there, I develop at least one goal for these four categories: personal, professional, family, and faith.

## 2023 Goals, Results, and Lessons Learned

The four goals from each focus area are:

Professional Goal: Exceed 10% profitability in the management company.

Background info on goal:

- The business has had some years with lower profitability and cash demands, especially in 2021 when I acquired a competitor. To free up the cash for the down payment of this acquisition (the rest was financed by a seller carry loan and an SBA loan), I had to sell one of my rental properties.

- I paid $900,000 for the business we acquired, which equated to roughly one times the business's revenue. I used the return on invested capital model Greg Crabtree outlined in Simple Numbers, Straight Talk, Big Profits to evaluate this deal. When I looked at the expenses, I could eliminate from that business by utilizing existing resources from my business and the possibility of growing the revenue by adopting our revenue model on the acquired company, it looked like we could generate about a 50% annual return on the capital invested after covering the cost to finance the rest. In reality, we churned more units after the sale than we had hoped, so I didn't quite hit this number. It was still profitable, and some of the employees from the acquired company continue to fill crucial roles.

- As the business has grown, I've had to build up more working capital, and I also want to pay off the loans I received. Both increasing reserves and paying off the principal of a loan are not reflected in the profit margin, so I know to get back to growing a real estate portfolio, I need the business to have the free cash flow for my investments.

- We were at 6.8% profitability in 2022, so this seemed like an attainable goal.

- This initiative involved working with a fractional CFO who helped us rebuild our forecasting model. I need to understand our revenue drivers more than I did heading into the year to feel like I'm in control of making choices to hit this goal. Property Management should be a relatively easy business to project. We know pretty accurately how many occupied units we will be managing, which will produce management fees each month, and we can estimate how many new properties we will bring on and need to lease, how many we will lose, how many tenants will move out, etc. However, it has been challenging sometimes to get as accurate as I would like as we have grown. There were times we would project a month with a $15,000 profit margin, but two or three of our revenue categories were off 5-10%. This, combined with some unexpected expenses, means we are quickly at break even for the month. Having a better understanding of these drivers allows us to set targets, make decisions along the way to support those targets, and hit them.

**Results:** I fell a little short on this one. We ended the year at 8% profitability. We certainly made some significant strides in our forecasting and understanding of some of the blind spots we had previously. I feel like we are on track to keep increasing our profit margin, but I didn't get there in 2023.

Family Goal: Go on at least one date night a month with my wife (family).

Background info on goal:

- We have three kids (ages 9, 7, and 3). It's a busy season of life, and we've struggled to find reliable babysitting. Finding new babysitters would be part of accomplishing the monthly date night.

- I enjoy spending time with my wife, Tara, but without setting intentions, it's easy to only schedule date nights around birthdays, Valentine's Day, and our anniversary. I knew that with some planning, this was very attainable.

**Results:** This was a big success. It ended up being easier than expected. Some of the highlights from the year:

- Friends of ours hosted a cocktail party with us and one additional couple. Each of us was responsible for making a cocktail, so we went all out on researching and sampling some options and bringing something very elevated. Unfortunately, my cocktail (Enzoni) came in last in voting; I'm really hoping for a rematch in 2024.

- Several of our friends had 40th birthday parties, which led to some nice dinners, a hotel stay, and other activities. This got both of us thinking a lot about how we want to celebrate our 40th birthdays in the next two years.

- We attended a paella party hosted by a former chef as part of a fundraiser for our kids' school. This was a unique and fun event.

- For my birthday, my wife bought tickets to see the Preservation Hall Jazz Band at the Denver Botanic Gardens. We had not been to a concert there before, and despite a rain delay, it was a great time enjoying a picnic dinner alongside the music and beautiful venue.

Faith Goal: Take a spiritual retreat.

Background info on goal:

- I struggle to make time for solitude and reflection. Again, having three young kids, life can be busy and full. Without some real intention, it's easy to go through the motions and not take time to pray and reflect.

- Several friends have taken similar retreats, perhaps once or twice a year, and shared how impactful they were for them. This led me to want to give it a try since I've not really done anything quite like it.

- My initial definition of this goal was to have at least two nights where I could get away and stay somewhere by myself. Some activities I wanted to include were fasting from food, a time for journaling and reflection, some guided prayer, and separation from my phone and similar distractions.

**Results:** I pivoted on this one. I have wanted to take a sabbatical for a couple of years. Early in the year, I realized that the team at Keyrenter was in a good place, and there was an opportunity to finally get away from work for a while. As a result, I was able to take 6 weeks away from work. Some of the highlights from my time off:

- I was able to do some fun activities, including:
    - Two camping/backpacking trips.
    - A trip to Saint Louis to see friends.
    - Six rounds of golf.
    - Several nice hikes, including a portion of the Colorado Trail and Bear Peak.
    - Lots of family time.
    - Two painting classes and a drawing class.

- o Started a streak of 10K steps a day that lasted 130 days.

- One lesson was that any transition from our everyday routines is challenging. Not going to work was a new rhythm for my family. Being clear on when I'd be around and when I'd be occupied was quite gray, so it took a few weeks to settle into making that work for everyone.

- The transition back to work and the following months have shown this time to be very transformative. Just the act of handing off all my work and then getting to decide what I take back and what is worth spending my time on has reshaped what I'm involved in on a weekly basis. I now serve more of a CEO role and have narrowed down my focus to higher-impact work rather than plugging all the holes that I just hadn't bothered or knew how to hand off before.

Personal Goal: Watercolor throughout the whole year.

Background info on goal:

- My sister recommended a workbook called The Artist's Way to me in 2022. I was hesitant, but her enthusiasm convinced me to try it. Reading it and completing the activities, I realized that I had really enjoyed my artistic pursuits as a kid. I had believed that my dad and sister were the artists of the family and my mom and I were the jocks. So, that belief had kept me from spending much time with art. After completing the workbook, I started playing with my kids' watercolor paints and found myself wanting to do more. I upgraded my supplies, and my wife bought me a six-week intro to watercolor class at the Art Students League of Denver, which began in January.

- I've had quite a few hobbies in my life, and sometimes, I can lose interest when I hit a plateau. However, I had a strong sense that I wanted to stick with this one and see if I could enjoy it as I improved. I defined the goal further by saying I needed to do at least one painting a week to satisfy my goal.

**Results:** This was a massive success for me. Some highlights:

- My dad had some watercolor experience from his time working as an architectural renderer and gave me many of his old supplies. The supplies were great, but even more so was the connection with him in sharing what I was working on. He was very eager to give feedback and encouragement. We ended up spending a day going to a gallery and the Denver Art Museum to talk about composition, mediums, and our opinions on styles and works. I did not anticipate this benefit from the goal. Still, it's been a really rewarding year of getting closer to him and growing a newfound appreciation of his knowledge and skill around art and drawing.

- There were periods when I felt like I wasn't getting any better, but overall, it was very rewarding. Doing this made me feel like some part of me came alive that I hadn't felt in a long time. I plan to keep learning and painting.

- If you are curious to see my work, I posted some of my favorite pieces I did in the year on my Instagram: https://www.instagram.com/brandonscholten/.

## 2024 Goals

I went through the same process as the year before in reflecting on where things currently stand with the life analytics tool to develop these goals for 2024. Feel free to email me if you want me to share the tool.

Professional Goal: Find a consistent way to contribute to marketing that lights me up.

Background info on goal:

- I see a lot of value in marketing fundamentals, specifically topics like lead magnets, funnels, drip campaigns, attribution, and conversion. I spend a reasonable amount of time helping develop the marketing strategy alongside our marketing manager and chief of staff. We plan to level up our analytics and infrastructure this year so we can better implement campaigns, measure what is working, and understand the return on investment.

- Next, I recognize that there are opportunities for me to network, build relationships, share my story, and overall represent Keyrenter through my own "personal brand," for lack of a better phrase. What I like about this aspect of marketing is that I can control what I want to spend my time on. I'm trying to shed any of the shoulds that I feel here and only pursue the few critical things that I really enjoy that fit into my natural gifts.

- A big part of this will involve a version of the "Dream 100" concept introduced in The Ultimate Sales Machine by the late Chet Holmes. The thesis is that there are always a smaller number of best buyers (or dream affiliates), and then there are total buyers. I've spent time on this in the past, but I've never pushed it forward consistently. I believe in further developing a targeted list and trusting that the people and companies I'm most excited about pursuing from that list are likely the ones I'll enjoy spending my time with and the most fruitful in terms of referrals and new clients.

- I know there will be a process of building a plan and then following through on it. I'm committed to thinking and reflecting early in the year, putting plans into action, and pivoting as needed. Most of all, I want to keep my focus this year on consistently pushing into the marketing opportunities that feel uniquely mine. Writing a chapter in this book is part of starting on this goal.

**Personal Goal: Take at least two backpacking trips of two or more nights.**

- Despite living in Colorado my whole life, it was not until last year, during my sabbatical, that I had my first backpacking trip. It was only one night and about an 8.5-mile hike round trip. I overpacked like a total beginner, which made the hiking quite painful, but I still loved it, and it gave me the bug to do it more. I spent the winter reading on gear and put together a basic lightweight setup to get started. I want to take the initiative this year to get out a couple of times. With three kids, I know my ambitions here are meager, but I think this goal is doable and will help me learn a lot and get a better feel for it.

- I'd love to do an epic backpacking trip with a handful of friends for my 40th birthday in 2025, but since I don't have any friends with lots of experience who can be the ones to organize, plan, and lead the trip, making sure to get out a couple of times this year will help prepare me to play that role.

- I would love to hear from any avid backpackers who would like a companion and can tolerate a newbie.

**Family Goal: Establish life-giving rhythms for managing personal finances.**

- This has historically been a big challenge for my wife and me. We've tried many available tools for tracking expenses and categorizing. Except for the first few years of marriage, when our income was significantly less, nothing has stuck for more than a few months. I always find some level of enthusiasm when we get started. However, the whole process quickly becomes drudgery and a source of conflict, and some nominal purchase is over-scrutinized.

- In other areas of life, I've found that it's often better to define what I am excited about and what I find helpful and valuable, rather than focusing on the negative side. We both strongly desire to spend money in a way that aligns with what we value, and to be responsible with our money so we don't put undue stress on ourselves in the future. I'm convinced that we can find a way of regularly looking at our expenses and reflecting that will generally be a positive experience and serve as a reminder of what's important to us and how we can adjust going forward when we've strayed from a path that makes sense to us.

- I plan to have many conversations with others about what they have found helpful in this area, try various tools or ways to approach it, and reflect knowing that we likely will not get it right on the first attempt. One idea I might pursue is finding a bookkeeper for a few hours a month, who could focus on personal finance, and prepare something for my wife and I to discuss. It will be important to stick with this throughout the year until we have found a methodology and rhythm that works well for us and that we can stick to.

## Faith Goal: Engage in a weekly small group.

- Since having kids, we have been members of two different churches, both of which had several hundred people attend multiple services. In this environment, it has been easy for us to attend a Sunday service each week but not really develop any meaningful connections.

- I've had several experiences in other seasons of life where I was part of a smaller group with much more profound relationships, where there was more room for vulnerability, intimacy, and community. I can see how much I grew and was shaped by those experiences, and we could benefit from finding that again.

- It's been quite a few years since we've had anything like this. We recently started going to a weekly group with several parents of kids who go to the same school as our kids, and I'm optimistic that if we stick with it, we can find that level of connection again.

- I find it easy to come up with excuses and let life get in the way, so I wanted to make this a goal that keeps us committed even when we have good reasons to skip it.

# Caitlin Logue

I was honored when Chris asked me to contribute his book.  Thank you, Chris!

Every real estate entrepreneur has to begin somewhere, and that's where I'm at -- the very beginning.  Lately, Frank Sinatra's "My Way" has been on repeat in my head.  It's a beautiful song about staying true to yourself.  He uses the phrase "My way" to describe his self-determination to carve his own path.  And that's what I'm going to do.

This year, I made a thoughtful and strategic move to leave my SaaS career and go full-time into real estate (more on this later).  I am humbly approaching this next chapter of my life, and I could not be more excited to share this journey with all of you!

## My background in SaaS

Why did I leave my SaaS career behind to go into real estate?

Let me tell you a story.

In 2022, I bought my first house—a cute little bungalow in Denver.  I got a decent rate—4.875%—and put 10% down.  I was excited because I was "building equity in my home," as everyone likes to tell you as a good reason for buying a house.  A couple of months into living there, this dream of owning a home soon became a nightmare.

It turned out to be one of the biggest financial mistakes I have ever made.

The neighborhood was completely unsafe.  This was a rookie mistake for a first-time home buyer, and I should have known better.

I ended up selling my house for what I bought it for.  I almost took a bath on it, but I got lucky with the timing of the market and a good buyer.

This entire experience inspired me to get my real estate license in Colorado.

My long-term goal is to become an accredited real estate investor. My first home-buying experience did not deter me from real estate; in fact, it did the opposite. It lit a fire in me to come back and do it better and smarter!

As part of that, I met Chris Lopez and joined the Property Llama team! Transferring my B2B SaaS sales into real estate has been a game changer for me, and I look forward to using those skills to help Property Llama grow exponentially.

## 2024 Goals

- Invest in my first passive real estate deal.

- Make my first real estate buy/sell transaction as a licensed agent.

- Help Property Llama grow and exceed revenue goals.

I'm keeping these goals super simple. I'm sure these will change throughout the year, so they could be entirely different next year. I'm OK with that.

## Connect with Caitlin

Caitlin Logue is a licensed agent who works with investors at Property Llama, helping connect real investors to deals across asset classes, sponsors, and geographies. Caitlin lives in Denver, CO, and loves connecting with people. You can reach her at caitlin@propertyllama.com or LinkedIn: https://www.linkedin.com/in/caitlin-logue/

# Chris Lawhead

Chris Lawhead is a farmland, multi-family, and debt investor. He has a lending practice serving investors big and small, from private loans to conventional financing. He's an author, a jiu-jitsu practitioner, and happily runs a music scholarship.

Connect with Chris at 303-929-8040 or Chris@AcresFirstLending.com AcresFirstLending.com

## About My Strategy

My big focuses are growth, income, service, and lifestyle.

My growth focuses on continuing my LP ladder. Like a bond ladder, my LP ladder goal is to invest in syndications or RE funds every year for 5 years. Then, in year 5, the first LP position matures and is closed. I take a distribution from the closing of that investment and reallocate it to another syndication or fund, hopefully continuing this ladder for many years.

For income, I'm investing in debt. Specifically, private loans to Real Estate Investors (flippers, farmers, ranchers, etc.). My company, Acres First Lending, focuses on short-term bridge loans collateralized by Real Estate that we understand and can confidently underwrite. Debt investments in private loans are more liquid than my multi-family fund investments and offer a more stable cash flow. I view debt investments as complementary to my growth strategy with syndications and funds. Debt offers income; syndications offer growth.

For service, I still love helping newer investors get started in Real Estate, primarily as a lender, but also as a mentor or sounding board. I've helped 17 people go from nothing to millionaire Real Estate Investors, and I'd love to see that number grow. I am contributing to the community with Property Llama, Bigger Pockets, and my own YouTube channel (Capital Stewardship). I hope to complete a few books that I have slowly been writing over the years: one on passive investing and the other on fraud detection and prevention.

Finally, my lifestyle is just as important as my income or portfolio growth. I pragmatically focus on health, wealth, love, and happiness, with the understanding that all are necessary for a good life. Community and relationships are the backbone of all the important categories in life. My jiu-jitsu community for health. My Real Estate community for wealth. My family and friends for love. And happiness is a byproduct of the previous three.

## 2023 Results and Lessons Learned

2023 was a wild year for me. I started a private lending company, Acres First Lending, which broadened my practice far beyond traditional financing. I became an employee again for the first time in 22 years in Private Equity. First as the head of Investor Relations at a real estate private equity company, and then again with Property Llama Capital with Chris Lopez. It was a great compliment that both these men believed in me. I made two Real Estate exits and sold a farm and a small apartment building. I started my LP ladder in a syndication and multi-family fund. I also completed a syndication I sponsored with excellent results.

2023 was a great learning year! I learned about depreciation shares in syndications and funds and how that was a better tax strategy for me over 1031 exchanges into bad deals (no tax advice here). I learned that certain sponsors are simply better at multi-family investing than I am, and I'd rather put money into their deals as opposed to sponsoring my own. I learned that investing my money, alongside my investors' money, in debt deals (private loans) is a great fit for my risk tolerance, Real Estate experience, and competencies. I also learned about the Property Llama software and became acutely aware of 'stale equity' and modeling for ROE (return on equity), thanks to Matt Amundson and Chris Lopez. I learned that I could hang intellectually with very smart businesspeople with fancy degrees from world-class schools. It turns out the School of Hard Knocks is as legit as MIT. I learned the level and sophistication of the fraudsters out there when my mom fell victim to a nasty scam. I learned more security measures to protect my data and money and how to protect my elderly mother from the vultures out there. I learned more about farmland than I thought possible with my friend and securities attorney, which led me to expand my lending practice to include farm and ranch land. Finally, I learned how adaptable I can be and that I still have a ton to learn about investing, capital stewardship, and fraud prevention. There's plenty of work ahead, which I'm grateful for.

## 2024 Goals

My big goals include earning a brown belt in Brazilian Jiu Jitsu, helping farmers and ranchers with bridge loans, and helping my network fund their Real Estate deals. I hope to add two multi-family syndications or funds to my LP ladder for growth. For income, I plan on investing in sound debt opportunities (private loans) secured by real estate. I hope to complete the books I've been working on: one on fraud prevention, the next on investing in debt, and the third on the fundamentals of passive investing in funds and syndications. I cannot hit any of these goals alone. I can only do all this with my amazing crew of partners, investors, contractors, consultants, friends, training partners, and family. Let us make 2024 amazing together!

# Chris Lopez

I found a recurring theme for 2023: PIVOT. The same mantra carries into 2024.

I'm excited to share my 2023 review and 2024 goals. Reviewing last year's goals is always an insightful exercise. Comparing my 2023 goals with the end-of-year results, you can clearly see the pivots I made. My 2024 goals reflect that I'm still pivoting with the market – follow the opportunities.

## 2023 Investing Goals Review

1. Buy another rental property. Because of the price points in Denver, I'll probably look in Colorado Springs or Pueblo—I did NOT accomplish this.

As we all know, with the interest rate spikes suppressing returns, the market didn't make much sense to acquire more properties. So, Pivot.

I ended up selling a rental I bought in 2021 for 15% down. While it was still a good-performing rental, the big appreciation phase had tapered off. I sold it in Q4 2023.

I invested the proceeds passively with Property Llama Capital's value add multi-family fund, utilizing a "lazy 1031 exchange" where the multi-family depreciation offset some of my capital gains and depreciation recapture.

2. Continue investing passively – Accomplished.

This was not a clear goal, but it became a bigger objective. Again, with the market shifting as it did, I chose to pivot and make this a more prominent focus. I didn't just shift my immediate investing strategy goals to be more passive; I started to look at it on a more macro level. I also started pivoting my 5-10 year goals to focus more on passive investing. Follow the trend!

# 2024 Investing Goals

1. Sell two rental properties in Q1.

Like the rental I sold in 2023, I've doubled my money, primarily through high market appreciation. I plan to sell high and reinvest the proceeds passively into commercial real estate via syndications and funds to buy low.

When I've told people about this plan, the immediate response is often, "Why are you selling cash-flowing rentals with debt below 4%?"

The return on equity (ROE) is 9.5%, about the same as historical stock market returns. If I'm dealing with the headaches and risks of rentals, I want a higher return than the stock market. My target ROE is 15%+.

Plus, the internal rate of return (IRR) goes down every year I hold onto it. IRR shows the annual returns over the investment's holding period, while ROE shows the estimated returns for the following year.

The condos are in the same complex. I purchased them for $195,000 and $207,000 in 2020 with a 25% down payment. Below is a graph showing the IRR if I sold them that year. The IRRs for both are very similar, so I took the average.

IRR for Condo Investments

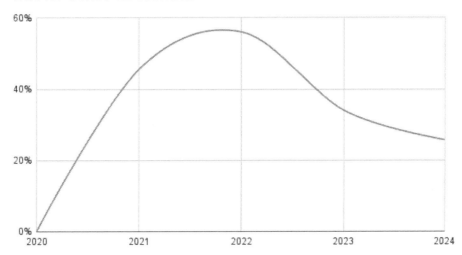

What do you notice about the IRR? It shot up in 2021 and 2022! Since the values peaked in 2022 and leveled off, IRR will start decreasing every year. I wish I could say it was from the value that I added. It's not. It was the gift of low interest rates that made the values dramatically increase. In markets like Denver, most returns have been through appreciation (equity gain), not cash flow. Since IRR takes into account the time value of money, it's no surprise the IRR is highest in the first two years.

**Four Scenarios**

Since the IRR has peaked and is declining, it was time to look at alternatives.

**Scenario #1: Keep it and Raise Rents by $500+**

Both units have had the same tenants for the last three years. They are great tenants, and I had no vacancy or turn costs by keeping them. However, my rents are below market by $250 per unit or about 8%.

Increasing the rents changes the ROE from 9.5% to 11.8%. A 2.3% bump is nice, but it's still below my 15% ROE baseline target.

**An interesting point is that a $500/mo increase in rents has a relatively low impact on IRR.** Below is a graph showing the IRR results over the next five years if I held onto the properties and increased them to market rent.

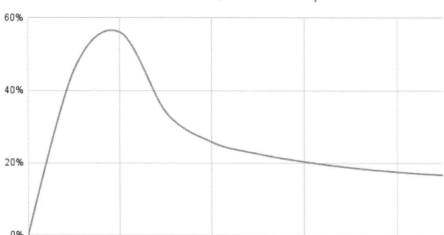

IRR for Condo Investments w/ $500 rent bump

**If I hold for 5 more years, the IRR will still go down!** Since so much of the return was front-loaded in the first two years, holding onto the properties will not improve the IRR.

The only way to tap into equity is to refinance or sell the property.

### Scenario #2: Cash Out Refinance

I've run this scenario and know the results. Refinancing does not work when interest rates are high. The interest rate on a 5% cap rate property will be in the 7-8% range. It'll end up being a negatively cash-flowing property.

### Scenario #3: Sell and 1031 Exchange into a Fourplex

Previously, I've had great success selling a condo and then doing a 1031 exchange into a fourplex. Let's look at purchasing a turnkey fourplex in Colorado Springs for

$750,000. It's a 5.8% cap rate with property management. It needs a 33% down payment with a 7% rate.

Here's a screenshot from a Property Llama scenario:

## Lopez 2 Condos w/ Rent Bump 2024

| | |
|---|---|
| Return on Equity | 11.87 % |
| Total Value | $ 550,000 |
| Total Equity | $ 272,000 |
| Annual Cashflow | $ 11,840 |
| Annual NOI | $ 27,912 |
| LTV | 50.55 % |
| Loan Balance | $ 278,000 |

### Year 1 Return Breakdown

Current Annual Return Breakdown

$32,298

- Appreciation  $ 11,000
- Debt Paydown  $ 6,724
- Cash Flow  $ 11,840
- Depreciation  $ 2,734

Show Current Annual Return Breakdown in Percents

- ✓ Highest Return on Equity
- ✓ Highest Net Worth · Equity
- ✓ Highest Annual Cashflow
- ✓ Lowest Loan to Value
- ⚊ Lowest Valuation
- ⚊ Lowest Annual Net Operating Income

## Colorado Springs fourplex 1031 upleg

| | |
|---|---|
| Return on Equity | 11.42 % |
| Total Value | $ 750,000 |
| Total Equity | $ 248,500 |
| Annual Cashflow | $ 3,097 |
| Annual NOI | $ 43,214 |
| LTV | 66.87 % |
| Loan Balance | $ 501,500 |

### Year 1 Return Breakdown

Current Annual Return Breakdown

$28,374

- Appreciation  $ 15,000
- Debt Paydown  $ 5,177
- Cash Flow  $ 3,097
- Depreciation  $ 5,100

Show Current Annual Return Breakdown in Percents

- ✓ Highest Rents
- ✓ Highest Valuation
- ✓ Highest Annual Net Operating Income
- ✓ Highest Loan to Value
- ✓ Highest Loan Balance
- ⚊ Lowest Return on Equity
- ⚊ Lowest Net Worth - Equity
- ⚊ Lowest Annual Cashflow

Analysis

- Return on equity decreases by 0.4%, which indicates a lateral move for growth.

- Cash flow decreases from $11,800 to $3,000!

- The high interest rates make it tough for 1031 exchanges. Pass on this scenario.

**Scenario #4: Sell and Lazy 1031 Exchange into Passive Deals**

Another reason the fourplex trade-up doesn't work is that prices haven't dropped. They have dropped in commercial multi-family and other commercial assets. Since I'm seeing the best returns with passive investing and less hassle, I'm doing a "Lazy 1031 exchange". This is a term I heard from Hall CPA.

Here's the process:

- Sell your property.

- Don't do a 1031 exchange.

- Invest in a rental (when you find the right deal) or in a passive investment with depreciation.

- The depreciation from the new investment will offset some of your capital gains and depreciation recapture.

| Proceeds | $230,000 | After all fees, closing costs, and loan payoff |
| --- | --- | --- |
| Reserves | $20,000 | Not owning rentals frees up the 6 months of cash reserves |
| Estimated Taxes | $40,000 | 22% estimated tax rate |
| Est Final Proceeds | $210,000 | |

If I did a traditional 1031 exchange, the $40,000 in taxes would be deferred. With a Lazy 1031 exchange, I want to reduce my taxes and find a better investment. I'm making three investments with the proceeds:

1. $101,000 in a multi-family value add fund. The depreciation savings should offset my taxes by $10,000 to $15,000 for my lazy 1031 strategy.

2. $70,000 into a private credit fund that funds short-term loans to real estate investors. I view debt funds as the new way to generate cash flow. Many are paying 8-12% per year.

3. $50,000 into a development investment for building single-family homes in the Denver metro area. The houses are in a great location. The size and prices are also around the median price point, fulfilling a significant need for more housing.

Why not invest all the proceeds into the multi-family value add fund for more depreciation? For diversification! Taxes are an important consideration but are not the only factor. Plus, these proceeds are invested with my overall portfolio in mind, which already has significant exposure to multi-family and more depreciation.

With the estimated multi-family tax savings, I'll have about $220,000 to invest. Here's a table to illustrate my projected returns:

| Investment | Amount | 2024 | 2025 | 2026 | 2027 | 2028 |
|---|---|---|---|---|---|---|
| **Multi-family value add fund** | $101,000 | -$40000 | $5000 | $6000 | $7000 | $188000 |
| Notes | | *depreciation loss | *cash flow | *cash flow | *cash flow | *sell/refi buildings |
| **Private credit fund (12%)** | $70,000 | $5,880 | $8,400 | $8,400 | $8,400 | $8,400 |
| 12% annual interest | | *Partial year | | | | |
| **Development opportunity** | $50,000 | 0 | $85,000 | | | $150,000 |
| Notes | | | *2 year exit, reinvest into another dev deal | | | *second dev deal paying out |

The timing of the return profile is very different from that of a typical rental. Hopefully, the above table clearly communicates the timing of the cash flows.

## Comparison in Five Years

I'm choosing scenario #4 of selling my rentals to invest passively. Here is my projected comparison over the next five years:

| | Rentals w/ $500 rent bump | Passive Portfolio | Difference |
|---|---|---|---|
| Cumulative cash flow | $40,200 | $57,480 | 43% |
| Total Equity | $284,000 | $408,000 | 30% |
| IRR | 16.7% | 22.5% | 35% |

Since I'm in growth mode, I'm more focused on equity growth, not cash flow. The passive portfolio is projected to generate more cash flow and equity growth while I have less hassle and liability.

**2. Roll over wife's 401k from old employer into a self-directed IRA Q1 to invest in real estate.**

I started investing in stocks long before investing in real estate. I've always kept a healthy portion of my capital in the stock market. However, I've consistently generated better returns over the last decade through real estate investing. So, I'm rebalancing my entire portfolio to have fewer stocks and invest in more real estate.

Because of market conditions and unfavorable lending restrictions, I won't use the IRA money to buy rentals directly. Instead, I'll invest passively, as outlined in the previous section.

**3. Sell Westminster Fourplex to 1031 Exchange Into a Bigger and Better Property.**

I've owned this fourplex for six years, and it has a low return on equity. Like the condo example, the IRR decreases every year. I want to sell to recycle my capital into a bigger and better deal. However, if there is no 1031 exchange, I'll have a big six-figure tax bill due to my low tax basis.

Since the fourplex has over $500,000 in equity, it opens up different 1031 options. The plan is to sell and utilize Property Llama Capital's 1031 exchange marketplace. I aim to keep the 1031 tax benefits and trade up into a bigger and better property!

## 2023 Business Goals Review

As an entrepreneur, I also had to make pivots. A lesson learned from my internet business is to not just pivot **but pivot fast** when trends change. I spent two years spinning my tires in my previous business before finally pivoting to real estate.

Those two years were my most miserable years as an entrepreneur. Grinding away with mediocre results is not good for the entrepreneurial soul.

I promised myself no entrepreneurial purgatory ever again! In early 2023, I felt the tires starting to spin some. What worked in the previous market cycle was no longer working; while my tires were spinning in some areas, others started getting traction elsewhere.

## Envision Advisors – Colorado Investor Friendly Agents

Envision Advisors has recently transitioned from a vertically integrated team model to a referral network of agents. Vertical integration was instrumental in our success, helping numerous investors buy and sell rental properties in Denver, Colorado Springs, and Pueblo. However, as we expanded geographically and brought on more agents, this model created operational friction that impeded our ability to source deals effectively in the changing market.

For Envision clients, this pivot represents an exciting opportunity rather than any cause for concern. The referral network model enables us to scale our geographic coverage across Colorado more efficiently while onboarding highly specialized agent partners. Our clients can expect an enhanced level of service and access to an even broader array of investment opportunities statewide.

We remain unwavering in our commitment to delivering exceptional results for our clients. This strategic shift positions Envision Advisors optimally to capitalize on future growth while maintaining our signature attentive service and market expertise. We look forward to continuing to build value for our investors through this client-centric approach.

## Property Llama

Property Llama is a software platform designed to help real estate investors track and analyze the performance of their investment portfolios while providing tools to optimize returns. In 2023, our primary focus was enhancing the investor dashboard experience and expanding our national reach.

The Property Llama platform underwent significant updates over the past year to improve investors' user experience. Key enhancements include additional portfolio comparison and scenario modeling capabilities and new features for tracking passive investments. We encourage users to create a free account or log in at www.PropertyLlama.com to explore these latest updates firsthand.

As 2023 came to a close, we made substantial progress towards our other goal of national expansion. Through strategic initiatives, we successfully onboard several hundred new investors nationwide each month on the Property Llama platform, with trends indicating continued growth.

In 2023, Property Llama raised capital from investors to fuel our software development and national scaling efforts. We are immensely grateful for the trust and support we have received from our investor partners and employees who have acquired stock options. This vote of confidence is a testament to the hard work of our co-founding team and energizes us for the exciting road ahead.

We plan to hold our inaugural Property Llama Annual Shareholder Meeting in Q1 2024. We are documenting our journey, so everyone is invited to contact us for details and access to the meeting recording.

## Property Llama Capital

The launch of our capital group, Property Llama Capital, in 2023 was not part of our initial goals for the year. However, it aligned with the overarching theme of strategic pivots. The decision to establish this new venture was driven by the realization that the most lucrative real estate opportunities lie within the commercial sector, coupled with a unique opportunity to curate deals for our valued investors.

Real Estate Sponsors face an increasing need for capital to fund their projects, and many are seeking to establish robust personal brands to facilitate scalability. These Sponsors have been reaching out to us, recognizing our proven ability to raise capital for their deals and leverage online media to amplify their brands. Few organizations possess the capabilities we offer to assist Sponsors in achieving their ambitious objectives.

This translates into a distinct advantage for our investors: **We are uniquely positioned to curate Sponsors with solid track records and structure favorable investment opportunities**.

Towards the end of 2023, we launched Property Llama Capital to structure passive investments for active landlords. Our deals also allow active investors to diversify their portfolios by incorporating investment-grade real estate assets.

### Fractional 1031 Exchange Market Place

From an active investor's perspective, we can structure deals differently than other capital groups. Many landlords appreciate the passive nature of investments but are deterred by the inability to perform a 1031 exchange into a syndication or fund. I'm pleased to announce that in 2024, we will launch our fractional 1031 exchange marketplace. It's the solution to investors' 1031 dilemma!

Investors will have the opportunity to sell their rental properties and then execute a 1031 exchange as tenants-in-common into larger deals. This will enable numerous investors to capitalize on the benefits while maintaining a hands-off approach. The key advantages include:

- Realizing the tax benefits of a 1031 exchange

- Investing in deals that pencil out favorably in today's market

- Remaining hands-off as a full-time sponsor manages the project

I personally plan to sell my Westminster fourplex and reinvest the proceeds into one of these fractional 1031 exchanges. It represents the optimal balance between maximizing returns on investment and minimizing administrative burdens and stress. This will allow me to dedicate more quality time to my family.

Stay tuned for further details on our fractional 1031 exchange marketplace and other lucrative investment opportunities. As I write this, we are in the early stages, but it's an exciting opportunity to explore and grow!

## Curtis St Media

Curtis St Media (CSM) was founded in 2021 to create educational content and network strategically to drive business growth for Envision Advisors, Property Llama, and other business ventures. However, the vision quickly expanded as Curtis St Media's expertise in marketing, technology, and content creation attracted interest from other businesses and people seeking high-quality services in these areas.

What began as an internal content engine has evolved into a thriving media company that partners with clients to elevate their brands and reach their target audiences through compelling storytelling and innovative digital strategies. Curtis St Media's core mission is to help people and businesses in the real estate investing industry harness the power of media to build authentic connections, establish thought leadership, and ultimately drive revenue growth.

2023 was an excellent year for Curtis St Media as we scaled up internally. The company prides itself on taking an individualized approach to every client engagement. The team invests time in understanding each client's unique brand voice, target audience, and business objectives. Armed with these insights, we craft tailored strategies that resonate authentically and drive measurable results. Curtis St Media empowers businesses to captivate their audience's attention and outshine competitors through visually stunning video content, search engine-optimized websites, and data-driven digital marketing campaigns. As the media landscape continues to shift, the company remains committed to continuously evolving its offerings, providing cutting-edge solutions that keep clients ahead of emerging trends and positioned for long-term success.

Looking ahead to 2024, Curtis St Media has set its sights on attracting more strategic clients where synergies can be found to drive growth across complementary businesses. By cultivating these synergistic relationships, Curtis St Media can leverage its expertise to unlock new opportunities for collaboration, cross-promotion, and shared success. The goal is to create an ecosystem of mutually beneficial partnerships that amplify each other's strengths, ultimately providing greater client value while propelling sustainable growth for all parties involved.

## Thank you!

A big thank you to my investors, clients, partners, team members, and everyone in the investing community.

To my investors, your trust and financial backing have fueled our growth and enabled us to turn ideas into reality.

To my team members, your hard work, passion, and commitment have been the driving force behind our success.

To our partners, your collaboration and shared values have strengthened our endeavors. And to the entire investing community, your insights, feedback, and enthusiasm have been invaluable.

Gratitude is not just important; it is the cornerstone of our achievements. Thank you for being a part of this incredible journey.

## Keep Working Harder AND Smarter

If you've read my chapters before, you know I always end on this saying. It's how I view my work ethic. I grind, day-in-day-out. While I love the grind, I want to make sure I'm always working towards the light at the end of the tunnel as quickly as possible.

To working smarter and working harder in 2024!

# Eric Garber

## 2023 Goals

Since I'm a returning author this year, I'll start with a refresh of my 2023 goals...including what really happened. Then, I'll share some key lessons learned and the 2024 goals. If you are interested in a comprehensive recap of my story, check out last year's chapter, my guest spot on Chris Lopez's podcast (Denver Real Estate Investing Podcast, Ep. 444) or reach out directly.

## Goals for 2023:

1. Continue to house hack my primary.

This went well – My current tenant has been a good one and he extended his lease another year with a 3% increase in rent.

2. Drive up fourplex rents by at least 5%, through better property management and by completing a landscaping project to improve curb appeal (and reduce maintenance).

This did not go well:

- I completed the landscaping project in the summer for ~$8K, which did improve curb appeal.

- My property manager retired, giving me only minimal notice. This left me scrambling to find and interview new PMs during a very busy time at my day job. Additionally, one unit came due during this time and sat vacant for nearly a month longer than it should have because of the PM transition process.

- The new PM got off to a rocky start, but I worked with the owner of the company to get everything worked out, and things are running decently smoothly right now.

- Due to the timing of the vacant unit and some struggles getting maintenance completed promptly (including a complete paint job), it ended up leasing for significantly less than the previous tenant, so rather than driving up rent 5%, they are actually down 1%.

    3. Invest in at least (1) new multifamily syndication.

This did not happen due to a combination of lack of compelling deals.

    4. Become a general partner in at least (1) multifamily syndication with the **Regency Investment Group.**

This did not happen due to Regency not finding a deal that met their criteria in 2023. They instead focused on asset management, to ensure maximum performance on existing deals.

    5. Contribute significantly to my taxable brokerage account - get ~10% closer to my long-term goal.

This did not happen due to the rise in interest rates. Rather than put more money into my brokerage, I actually liquidated it to pay down 70% of my HELOC, which had doubled from 4.5% to 9% APR. While I wasn't excited about this move, I believe it was the right one. The HELOC was an intentional arbitrage play in order to leverage equity in my primary to invest in additional syndications that made a lot of sense at 4-6% APR, but a guaranteed 9% return is not something to take lightly. As I sell my current syndication investments, I will return big chunks of capital by allocating more of it to the brokerage to achieve the goal balance.

    6. Continue to max out my Roth 401K and HSA.

This was accomplished.

    7. Build up my emergency fund - to a full (6) months of expenses

This was accomplished.

## Other notable things that occurred in 2023:

1. I was a guest on two podcasts: Chris Lopez's and BiggerPockets Money. Being a guest on my first podcast was really interesting and challenging. I was also surprised at how different and unique each experience was.

2. I attended my first big commercial real estate conference/mastermind with J. Scott Scheel's Commercial Academy. This was a unique opportunity my friends at Regency Investment Group were able to provide by bringing me as their guest. The experience really opened my eyes to other real estate asset classes outside of residential, and I met some great people.

3. I completed a big project at my day job and landed a new, larger project that came with a promotion.

## Current Position at the end of 2023

- Primary house hack - performing well.

- Fourplex – still underperforming.

- Limited partner in (7) multifamily syndications across CO and TX (please reach out if you'd like to chat specifics).

- Taxable brokerage account – on hold as described previously.

- 401K/Roth 401K/HSA accounts are on pace to my Coast Financial Independence (Coast FI) goal.

- HELOC at 9% APR anticipated to be paid off in 1-2 years.

- Healthy emergency fund with at least (6) months of expenses.

# Lessons Learned in 2023

One of my favorite things about reading this book each year is the opportunity to learn from others' experiences. For that reason, I'll return the favor by sharing a few of the key lessons I learned from the year.

1. When interviewing property managers for the fourplex, one really impressed me. During our initial phone call, I was providing a summary of the rent roll, when she stopped me, and the following conversation occurred [to the best of my recollection]:

PM: "Why do you have leases ending in October?"

Me: "They weren't always that way, but as they've turned over and had some vacancy, they keep bumping out as new 12-month leases are signed"

PM: "That's dumb." [It's possible she didn't actually say this, but she may as well have]

Me: "What?"

PM: "I only write leases that end in the summer. It's the only way to minimize vacancy and maximize rent revenue."

While I think we all know that summer is the best time to lease units, how many of us are writing leases to ensure it happens *every* time at your units? None of my PMs were doing this at the fourplex, but now they are! I have applied this concept to my house hack, too.

2. At the Commercial Academy, my eyes were opened to the full breadth of commercial real estate investing opportunities. The mastermind had an interesting mix of broader education, real-life case studies/portfolio reviews, and networking. While I was able to learn a ton about retail, industrial, multifamily, etc., and meet a lot of great people, the biggest single lesson

learned from this event was this: *I could benefit greatly by removing some of my personal limiting beliefs.*

The discussion around removing limiting beliefs probably needs to be an entire chapter, but to summarize:

I realized that when I set personal goals and identify strategies to achieve those goals, I apply too many constraints. By opening up the aperture to what is possible and limiting these constraints, I may be able to meet my goals much quicker. I'd encourage you to ask yourself the same question as you think about how you will attack your goals – if you removed all of the constraints (e.g., job, location, living situation, asset class, etc.), what would the quickest path to meet your goals look like?

3.  Understanding the path of least resistance for improving your financial situation is extremely important and powerful. The key here is it allows you to focus on the most impactful thing first, or in simplest terms:  prioritizing. A simple example is if your job compensation includes sales commissions, you'd want to look at how many hours you need to spend to reasonably expect another big sale versus how much time you'd need to spend to earn that same amount on a side hustle.

As real estate transactions were grinding to a halt in 2023, with interest rates only expected to increase further, I found myself on the hunt for the next project at work. I realized that it might be a slow year on the real estate front, but now I had the opportunity to position myself for a promotion if I could find the right-sized project. Utilizing my network and some fortunate timing, I landed myself a significantly larger project and earned a promotion, resulting in a raise.

4.  At Pine Financial's annual Denver Real Estate Investor Success Summit, I listened to an eye-opening presentation from Eric Ross of Ecospace Property Management. While there was a lot of great information around the recent

tenant law changes in CO, there was one big shocker for me: Zillow background checks don't work in CO [many others in addition to Zillow don't work either]. In other words, Zillow will provide you with a report that shows people with felonies are clear.

I did some research, reading the details on Zillow's website, and there was no indication that the background check would not provide accurate results; it was simply a link to their provider, CIC. Following that link, I read CIC's details and again, no indication that the service will tell you that a convicted felon has a clear background. If you are performing background checks, research to ensure you are getting accurate results from your provider. Also, know that the Colorado Bureau of Investigation (CBI) provides a background check service.

## 2024 Goals

In order to contextualize the 2024 goals, I'll re-share my long-term goals:

- WHAT: Enjoy a low-risk, early retirement - by age 50.

- HOW: Create a cash flow to replace my W-2 job, bridging to when I can access retirement accounts

    o The number wiggles a bit, but is currently set at $8K/month (post-tax) in today's dollars or $10K/month (post-tax at 50 assuming average 4% inflation).

    o Utilize diversification of income sources to minimize risk - create a 50/50 diversified stock/real estate portfolio to satisfy income need of roughly $13K/month (pre-tax) with margin*

        ▪ Build a syndication ladder of $150K/year (invested) - creating a cash flow of roughly $11K/month (pre-tax)**.

        ▪ Fourplex - estimating a future cash flow of $1K/month (pre-tax).

- After-tax brokerage - estimating it could cover up to $3K/month (pre-tax).

*The 50/50 stock to real estate allocation includes my 401K/Roth/HSA accounts, which is why the early retirement income does not look balanced between stocks and real estate even though my entire portfolio goal is balanced.

**A syndication ladder is my strategy of investing in new syndication deals each year and was detailed in last year's chapter – reach out if want to talk about this concept further.

## Goals for 2024:

1. Continue to house hack my primary.

2. Drive up fourplex rents at least 5%, through good property management and smart updates (such as fresh paint when units turn).

3. Become a general partner in at least (1) multifamily syndication.

4. Either pay off 50% of the remaining HELOC balance if interest rates stay flat or contribute to my taxable brokerage account if interest rates drop significantly.

5. Continue to max out my Roth 401K and HSA.

## About Me

Eric Garber has a 20+ year career in aerospace and is currently working to achieve FIRE through a mix of stock investing, house hacking, multifamily syndications and directly owned real estate investing. Eric is also an 'Investor Advocate' at the Regency Investment Group and is passionate about passive investing and values-based goal setting.

Connect with Eric at eric@regencyinvestmentgroup.com to discuss.

# Heidi Jensen

## My Real Estate Journey: From Family Traditions to Unique Airbnb Experiences

## Introduction:

I am a third-generation Coloradoan. My grandmother bought her first investment property in Grand Lake for a whopping $7000. Homes and home building are in my blood. My father, like his father before him, was a custom home designer and builder. Some of my earliest memories are going to vacant lots to find property lines. I remember being bored to tears, but I have realized that I learned so much during that time.

## Early Experiences:

My father won awards for his home designs in Boulder County and was acquiring investment properties, fix and flips, and vacant land. He was doing this without any training or knowledge about investing, just using his skill to do what he knew how to do best: build and fix. This was all before 2008, and things were looking good. He had gone to an investing meeting and happened across someone who was selling a property next to the University of Colorado Hospital. The property was in a difficult area of town, but he thought he would be able to sell it to a developer in short order. It was a nightmare property to start with, and then 2008 hit, and it all went belly up. In what felt like no time at all, my parents lost all the properties except two, one being their primary.

## Overcoming Fears and Taking Risks:

The impact of witnessing my parents' real estate struggles could have deterred me, but in 2019, I decided to embrace the opportunity. I convinced my parents to let me transform the bottom level of their house into an Airbnb. The immediate success of this endeavor was remarkable - in the first year, we not only covered the mortgage but also generated a minimum of $1,000 extra per month. Additionally, in the same year, I listed an arbitrage property on Airbnb, which brings in an average Cash-on-Cash Return (COCR) of 28.5%.

## Expanding the Portfolio:

- 2012 Bought first home to rent as a LTR.

- 2019 Listed the House Hack on Airbnb with a 28.5% (Cash-on-Cash Return) COCR.

- 2020: Listed an arbitrage property on Airbnb, achieving an average COCR of 28.5%.

- 2021: Acquired a cabin along a picturesque river. Previously managed with manual bookings and only accepting cash or checks, the property underwent updates. It currently boasts an impressive 41.6% COCR, reflecting the successful transition to modern booking methods and strategic improvements.

- 2022: I purchased a property on a Michigan lake, consistently generating a cash flow of at least 4x. While financially successful, this property was a labor of love, as I invested a lot of personal time and resources into remodeling it.

- 2023 Purchased single-family home for LTR in Colorado.

- 2024 Purchased 2 bedroom home in Midwest for a MTR, currently being furnished as I write.

## Shifting Strategies:

All my properties have operated as Airbnb units, but recognizing the changing landscape in the industry, I am now transitioning to a more tailored approach and have been focusing more and more on the comfort and experience of the guest. Going forward, I'll focus on creating unique experiences, one of my passions; I aim to differentiate my Airbnb offerings to create a stay that will be remembered for a lifetime. Additionally, considering the patience and consideration required for this approach, I am exploring opportunities in multi-family units that I will convert to a mixture of mid-term and long-term rentals.

## 2024 Goals

- BRRRR Four Multifamily Properties of various sizes.
    - Create a list of reputable GCs and subcontractors.
    - Find cash investors.
    - Finish creating a pitch deck for investors.
    - Develop a system for having an influx of investors that we can go to and their profiles, so we know which.
- Fine-tune my bookkeeping systems and practices.
    - Train my sister in bookkeeping so that she can take over the financials.
    - Spend 1x per week listening to REI tax strategy podcast.
- Create an SOP for my properties.
    - I have several properties for which I haven't yet created standard operating procedures. In Q1, I would like to create a breakdown of cleaning tasks.
    - Create a Google Doc SOP for what needs to be done at each property and when.
    - Create a step-by-step process for renovations, creating a duplicatable system.
- Get featured on a Podcast.

- This one is just for fun. I'd love to help other investors and hear from other investors who are doing what they love.

## Conclusion

2024 is going to be my year of growth. I've already bought one house this year, and as I get further into the community of investors and look at all the open doors, I know I only have to choose where to go. I will lean on my family's past construction and custom home-building knowledge. While I'm well on my way in my journey, this next year is the time for me to take my skills further and start giving back. Real Estate hasn't been the easiest path or the only one I have explored. But I know that this is what I love and enjoy doing. I wouldn't be where I am today without the knowledge, the failures, and the inspiration of others.

## Connect With Heidi

Heidi Jensen is an investor who continues her father's legacy. She manages construction projects and rehabs in the Denver area and specializes in fix-and-flips in the Midwest. She is a partner in Moirai Investments, managing and delivering quality multifamily flips.

# Jake Cohen

Jake Cohen is a real estate investor specializing in short-term rentals and owns Step By Step BNB, a short-term rental revenue management company. Essentially, I help people price their Airbnb properties to earn maximum revenue.

Connect with Jake at (720)-204-8727 or Jake@stepbystepbnb.com or www.stepbystepbnb.com.

## About My Strategy

My strategy in real estate investing has been an exercise in finding market inefficiencies and exploiting them. Over the years, this has included House Hacking, long-term rentals, and multi-family investing, and now, I focus mainly on short-term and mid-term rental investing.

Many new investors will chase the hot thing in the market, and I think we can always be susceptible to getting wrapped up in the hype of one thing or another. I have tried to look at the data subjectively and not go too deep down a rabbit hole unless the numbers warrant further investigation. By the time most of us hear of the next hot thing, the time to invest in that hot thing has already passed. So, instead of trying to hop on a bandwagon each time a new great thing comes along, I encourage getting really good at one thing that you like to do. I love numbers, and finding ways to make the numbers work for me is how I have done well in real estate thus far. You can often find a niche others aren't looking at and find tremendous success. I found this when buying multi-family properties, especially when everyone in the area was buying single-family or condos.

My current focus is on continuing to build my short-term rental business, which consists of a triplex in Steamboat Springs, CO & a duplex in Gulf Shores, AL. These properties have done very well for me. Still, I am now at the point where I want to make sure I am running these properties as efficiently as possible and working towards making them the best possible version of themselves. I bought my triplex in 2017, and while we did a significant renovation, I realized I could improve some aspects of the property. I added a hot tub this year and recognized the market has a lot of 2 & 3 bedroom units but very few larger units, so I am exploring renting the whole 7 bedrooms at once instead of as individual units. This will come with more renovations and a renewed focus on design to make it stand out from the pack.

I also made a significant pivot in my business this year. If you have read this book a couple of years in a row, you know I was working on growing a Short-Term Rental Course & Group Coaching. It did not turn out to be the path I wanted to take. So, this year, I experimented in a few other directions. I held an in-person Mastermind Group at my properties in Steamboat Springs, hosted a virtual mastermind with Zeona McIntyre, and started experimenting with a revenue management business for short-term rentals. I found that revenue management was the right path forward. In the past 4 months, I have onboarded about 40 listings and am seeing fabulous results in all parts of the country.

## 2023 Goals, Results, and Lessons Learned

1. In 2022, my family purchased a new house in Steamboat Springs. We spent much of the summer renovating and are about 90% complete with our project. This included new windows, siding, gutters, flooring, 2.5 bathroom remodels, new kitchen, new paint, updating electric & plumbing, correcting negative slope causing drainage problems at the front of our house, and lots of small items along the way. While this was a massive project, it was worth it. I estimate we increased the value by about $600,000 and spent about half that.

2. Our previous primary in Lakewood, CO, was a mid-term rental in 2022, but it didn't make as much money as we had hoped, so we

sold it in May 2023 and even got an offer over asking. This money was used to renovate our house in Steamboat.

3. I was hoping to have some money left over after our renovations to invest in a syndication fund, but we used it all and a few bucks from my retirement account instead. I did help my mom invest in a syndication fund, so I feel I got the education and understanding I was looking for.

4. Pulling money out of one of our current properties seemed like the best way to grow our STR business, but the more we considered it, the more it did not make sense, given the interest rates.

5. We did not buy another property in 2023 as planned.

6. I planned to expand my cohosting business further in 2023, but the revenue management business came out on top. I will finish the season in April 2024 with my cohosting clients and then focus on revenue management instead.

7. Revenue from our STR properties was up 0.1% last year. A win is a win!

8. My goal for cash flow from our rentals was also achieved due to less maintenance and capital expense costs.

9. One of my goals in 2023 was to join a group of like-minded people to share experiences throughout the year. I am in the Build Short-Term Rental Wealth Mastermind and have found my tribe. Great people are all working towards being great hosts! I look forward to continuing this path.

## 2024 Goals

1. Who not How! If you have not read this book, it is excellent; this is my mantra for this year. Find the person who can solve the problem instead of

trying to learn how to solve the problem yourself. I can't wait to see all the fantastic people who will come into my life by changing this mindset.

2. Along with this change, I will start to step away from the day-to-day running of my businesses to work on projects like new properties and ways to grow the revenue management business going forward.

3. Pumpkin Plan is another amazing book. You can only grow the biggest pumpkin once you trim away the seeds holding you back. I am in the process of trimming these parts of my life away. It includes:

    a. A long-term renter in our apartment at our primary has become too needy and complains about everything. Feb. 10th, move out!

    b. I am removing myself from the mastermind I started. This is complete as of Jan. 25th. This will give me time to focus on what I want to grow now.

    c. Passing on my cohosting clients to another person. April 2024.

    d. Trimming my revenue management clients to be the right people to work with. Already complete.

    e. These changes will give me the time to move on to more productive items in my life.

4. Transition 1 property to a Super Property. This could be upgrading our property in Steamboat to be a 7 bedroom masterpiece, selling our mid-term rental in Denver and purchasing something we would use long term, or selling our place in Gulf Shores and buying or building a beachfront property. I don't know which will happen, but I want at least one to happen this year.

5. Start a podcast! I have been told I have a face for Radio, and I figure a podcast could be my place in life. I look forward to trying this new adventure.

6. Add Syndications to my list of Real Estate Investments.

# James Brown

## About Me

I caught the real estate investing bug when I realized its true power to transform my life. I also love infecting friends, family, and clients with the disease.

Connect with James at https://linktr.ee/partnerwithjamesbrown.

## Introduction

I thought "Shiny Object Syndrome" would eventually go away when I first started in real estate. I know many people experience the same challenge because there are many ways to make money in real estate. This book isn't necessarily going to help this condition! My business partner Toby Hanson and I still struggle with it. Still, we also realize that markets are different, markets shift over time, and some seemingly different strategies can be complementary and powerful when combined. Combining strategies can protect you from downsides and take advantage of upsides. We understand there are risks in all kinds of investing, and we can make tons of money quickly, but we, and other investors we partner with, say that it is paramount to focus on safety, security, and long-term growth. We'll leave the high-risk stuff to other people with stomachs for that.

## Hybrid Investing

Hybrid Real Estate Investing is what we call the ways we invest in single-family homes using lease options (aka Rent-to-Own) as a medium-term exit strategy. We get cash upfront from our resident buyers. Then we get monthly cash flow from rent and cash later when our residents get a bank loan to buy the home and cash us out. In the past, we exclusively focused on "buyer-first," where we find buyers who cannot get a traditional loan, and we buy homes for them. We still use that model because we get more up-front and have little to no vacancy risk. The problem is that we needed to find more of those buyers consistently, so we added a proven property-first model because we can buy as many as we and our passive capital investors want. We can find more buyers since we require less down but still enough for them to have skin in the game. What we like about it is we avoid doing risky remodels with high holding costs, dealing with contractors, or dealing with regular renters who do not have much skin in the game or the intention of becoming homeowners. We also reduce typical vacancy risk, capital expenses like maintenance and repairs, and property management expenses. Our returns are better than regular rentals, too. Plus, we are helping deserving people become homeowners. There's a lot more I could go into, but those are some of the highlights.

## Alternative Asset Investing

We love our Hybrid investing model, but we also like other asset classes for different reasons. Simply diversifying within real estate is one reason. Another is that we need to have a full 20% down and the ability to get financing for the rest when we buy on-market, which is limiting. Of course, there are other ways to finance, like seller financing, buying subject-to-existing loans, finding assumable loans, and DSCR loans. Sometimes, we may just want to invest using the cash from our IRAs, home equity, or insurance policies for a straight return on debt without needing to qualify for a loan or put down $100k or more for a 20% down payment. So, we partner with experienced operators (GPs, aka General Partners) in real estate syndications. These operators are experts in buying, adding value, and operating specific asset classes like multifamily complexes (apartments) and have a track record in that space. Other asset classes we like are self-storage, mobile home parks, and RV parks. We are not exclusive to Colorado, but if the numbers work, of course, we'd like to have them here because we know, love, and believe in the long-term health of the market in Colorado.

# Partnerships

We have formed partnerships to have "Family Office" level advisory support without having the full-time staff typically only in place for ultra-wealthy families. As the saying goes, "Your network is your net worth."

**Fund Managers:** We are working with high-level fund managers with a track record of getting double-digit returns with low treasury-level risk. They did even better during the last recession! I have much to learn about how they do it, but that's the beautiful thing about partnering with people. We don't have to know it all to be successful.

**Trust Experts:** We work with a team that has 40 years of experience setting up trust structures designed and proven to provide tax savings, tax deferment, and asset protection. In the past, only the ultra-wealthy typically knew about or could afford to set these up and properly use them. We also like it because we never have to do a 1031 exchange again!

**Infinite Banking Experts:** Also known as "Bank on Yourself," this tool allows us to leverage the value of dividend-paying permanent life insurance policies. It's a strategy that has become highly refined over the years to use specifically for real estate investing because the cash value is protected and liquid. We don't have to wait for banks to approve loans or deal with underwriting. And the money in the account is always compounding.

# Shows

2024 will be the second full year I will host the "This Month in Real Estate Investing" show. I get to share and learn from a panel of three other experienced investors, and we talk about a wide variety of investing strategies, asset classes, and markets that appear in the news. I'll also continue to be a guest on other shows where I primarily share our Hybrid investing model. A big part of investing is constantly learning, so hosting the show and being a guest on other shows helps keep me on my toes.

## Meetups

Starting in December 2023, we joined forces with some other movers and shakers to launch the Colorado Cash-Flow Club - part of the nationwide Cash-Flow Breakfast Club. It will be very dynamic, with various speakers, strategies, action-oriented exercises, and interactive networking. It's vital for building solid relationships and authority as a leader in the industry.

## Content

I plan to create and post more video content, sharing my knowledge with anyone who wants to join me on this exciting journey.

# Jamin Cook

Jamin Cook is a Firefighter/Paramedic who converted to a realtor with aspirations of starting an investment portfolio in 2024.

Connect with Jamin at (720) 301-0761 or email at fireonfireinvesting@gmail.com

## Introduction

In 2020, I took a risk and started operating outside the comfort zone of the fire department. I got my real estate license. I had some successes and some failures in my first year, but I learned a lot from all of it.

In 2023, I started having conversations with one of my mentors, Paul DeSalvo. We wanted to teach first responders how to prepare financially for their future. Fire On Fire was born with guidance from Chris Lopez and his network.

## Strategy and Goals

- I have learned throughout my adult life that networking is a big part of success. I continue to network and will always strive to learn something new. I will always try to give back to my network.

- As a new emergency medical technician working for Flight For Life, I discovered a lot I didn't know. I would go down to the emergency room at St. Anthony Central between calls. I would offer to take patients to x-ray or clean rooms so the next patient could move into that room. This was not what I got into emergency medicine for, but I discovered early in my career that being willing to do the "dirty jobs" earned you respect, and in exchange, the nurses and doctors would go out of their way to teach me. This education was paramount to my success as a paramedic, and I have carried this knowledge throughout my career. So be willing to do the "dirty work"; let the education and respect you acquire be your reward! This will set you up for the future.

- I have one personal goal for 2024: investing in my first rental property! Buying a primary home is a no-brainer, and we typically don't stress as much about the risk with this investment.  Most of us invest in the stock market through a retirement plan without thinking twice because we have been taught to do this.  The fear of leaping real estate investing is not something we are taught, but it is one of the greatest ways to build wealth.  Fear of failing when others depend on me has been my hurdle.  Surrounding myself with smarter people and learning to evaluate an investment has been the best thing for my wife and I. Find your people!

- Build Fire On Fire to a state-wide first-responder networking group.  Help first responders and their families be prepared for retirement or in case they ever get injured and can't return to work.

- Travel, this is something I haven't done a lot of.  I have always been focused on work.  I want to take care of the person who supports me the most.  My wife is my biggest cheerleader, and I want to create memories and successes together.

# Jared Carlson

Jared Carlson is an investor-friendly real estate agent with Your Castle Real Estate. He helps other investors build their rental portfolios and has been consistently investing in buy-and-hold rental properties since 2012.

Connect with Jared at 303-596-9187 or [Jared@JaredCarlsonRealEstate.com.](mailto:Jared@JaredCarlsonRealEstate.com)

## About My Strategy

Let me rewind back to 2004. I left my W2 job with a production builder to start a construction home-building business, and with that, I had contributed to a 401K during my W2 years, and it needed to roll over to another account, which I did. As the years went on, starting a business didn't allow me to have much excess to keep contributing to a retirement fund, so my 401K funds sat idle for years. Then I dabbled with some money managers for a few years, and come 2010 or 2011, my funds were almost exactly the same as 2004!

I knew I needed to take control of my investing myself. In 2006, I got my real estate license and went full-time into real estate in 2009, when the market was crashing, but I also learned about self-directed IRAs. I had bought and sold a few rentals along the way, never any that I wanted to keep long-term, but I had $110K sitting in an IRA, not doing anything. As I was growing my real estate business, I also learned to invest in real estate within my IRA.

With an IRA investment, you have to put down 35% plus other fees, so I used up my $110K on 2 properties in 2012. I got serious real quick because I could see how the numbers worked out. As I stabilized the properties, I refinanced and bought 2 more and was also doing a Roth conversion with one of the properties. Fast-forward to 2023, and I had 4 properties within my IRA and 3 properties outside my IRA.

Now, to my current strategy

Actually, since 2012, my strategy has been the same.

1. Make sure I don't overleverage myself. Except for the first two properties where I used up all my funds, I want a sense of comfort so I can sleep at night knowing that I'm not overleveraged to the point where one water heater will cause significant issues to our finances. We've been successful on the financial end, but I do self-manage our properties, and I'm lucky to be able to do many of the repairs myself, so I do trade time for cost savings in many cases.

2. I am still in growth mode in terms of our investing, but that doesn't mean I'm growing to a massive number of properties. My goal has always been $10K/month, and it's a matter of managing the right properties and the right number of properties to achieve this.

3. Lastly, I don't mix our personal finances with the properties. Of course, there may be situations here and there, but overall, my goal is to have the properties operate as their own businesses. This allows us to make sure we have our own personal budget separate from the investments.

## 2023 Goals, Results, and Lessons Learned

Real Estate Investing Goals:

In late 2022, I was turning over one property to a new tenant and had one property turn over after a 10-year tenant left. That was good and bad. Good, I had a tenant that long, but bad because the property needed a major overhaul since I didn't do much when I bought it. I got the first property re-rented and continued to rehab the 2nd. That went into 2023, and then another property went vacant, so that had to be gone through. And then a 4th property was going to turn over shortly after that. This wasn't the norm for me; it just happened to pile up at once, but everyone gave me sufficient notice.

In 2022, I started learning about passive investing through private equity real estate funds, so I thought this would be a good time to pivot with a few properties.

2023 Goals—Our goals changed quickly from late 2022, but we set out to sell 2 of our properties outside my IRA and 1 property within my IRA. Then, we would take those proceeds and reinvest them passively. The sale of the 3 properties went extremely well, and we were able to reinvest them into two different real estate funds. It was a good year of execution.

## 2024 Goals

Personal Goals:

1. I have gotten away from taking care of myself, and I am feeling it! It's time to get back to exercise and eating better.

2. We have our 2 daughters in college, so helping them with the cost of school is a big goal this year.

3. Since we have 2 kids in college, my wife and I are trying to figure out what life is like. Work in progress.

Real Estate Agent Goals:

1. Grow my real estate transactions by 30% this year.

2. Put better systems in place and track my productivity.

3. consistency!

Investing Goals:

With our moves last year, we have a good chance of exceeding our initial monthly income goal, so we'll focus on analyzing our portfolio to avoid overleverage and maximize our opportunities this year.

This also may be a resting year. I am currently wrapping up some minor work on a property we're going to re-rent, and we have another lease coming due in May. We may just sit tight on our passive and active investments and not make any moves. But if we do make a move, it would be to sell one property and invest passively. We'll have to wait and see.

# Jeff Giesen

## About Me

Jeff Giesen is a real estate developer and investor focused on finding and funding new development projects. He has a background in technology leadership, program and project management, and process optimization. In the constant pursuit of learning, he is open to networking, partnering, sharing information, and trying new things.

Connect with Jeff at 720-317-4763 or giesen@giesenhouse.org.

## Pre-2024

To give some background, I bought my first real estate investment in 2011. It was a 2 bed, 2 bath, 1600 total sq. ft. empty duplex in Englewood that was on the MLS and bank owned. At 800 sq. ft. per side, they were sizable one-bedroom units complete with 1950s pink appliances and metal-trimmed pink Formica countertops. Quite the modern design – at that time! Outside was an unused, 2-spot carport sitting equally across the neighboring property line with a wall between the stalls, a workable space in the back yard with alley access, and a front yard with a sprinkler system. Some pretty good bones to work with.

Kitchen replacements, bath replacements, ceramic tile replacing linoleum flooring in those locations, refinished hardwoods formerly covered by carpet in the rest of the units, new windows, the typical Federal Pacific breaker box replacement, and a fresh coat of paint throughout rounded out most of the notable interior upgrades. On the outside, fresh paint, new gutters, sprinkler system fixes, a new 2 car garage with separate doors, and the creation of 8x8 ft enclosed storage units for each side by walling in the carport and voila, a rentable duplex was made. I really enjoyed that transformation process!

Fast forward to 2021, 10 years of the same two renters, not steady enough rent increases, general maintenance/repairs done mainly by myself, a crazy amount of market appreciation, raising children, having a day job, and a realization that I had fallen asleep at the wheel of my real estate investing. As I had done in 2010 and 2011, I returned to several real estate events and meetups I used to attend to reacquaint myself with the current investing market. One such event was the yearly Investors Success Summit. Two things happened at this event.

First, I attended a Return on Equity (ROE) session. We did not get past the first example in the presentation, and I had the sinking realization that I had a problem - and by problem, I do not necessarily mean it was a bad thing! The presenter of the session was Chris Lopez, who offered a free consultation to the attendees to go over our individual scenarios. Sure enough, we plugged my numbers into his spreadsheet, and it screamed, "DO SOMETHING!". I had way too much equity that needed to be working harder. The most prudent options for a single-digit ROE were to either take out a ton of the equity and redeploy it or sell the property outright.

The second thing that happened at the summit was that I was introduced to Nathan Adams of redT Homes. Throughout the area of Englewood where my duplex was located, I continued to see new, two to three-story, side-by-side duplexes, triplexes, and even fourplexes with rooftop decks replacing older homes selling at stellar prices. Wow, I wanted to do that! To take a thing and create something new and great excites me. As a kid, I loved to watch and tour new homes as they were built in my neighborhood. For someone with a day job in the tech industry and no real entitlement or construction background to speak of, I thought pursuing a project like that was out of reach. Then, I was pointed to Nathan.

After determining the location of my duplex was not ideal for a scrape, we decided that I should upgrade and outright sell. I took that approach but did not go quite that simple. I worked with the city over a much too elongated timeframe to establish the units as condos so that they could be sold individually. This created an ownership opportunity for two buyers at a price point not commonly seen in the market at the time and a way to maximize my return. In 2023, both units were sold. I learned a lot working with the city on entitlements, and once again, I really enjoyed the transformation process!

While working on the duplex process, I began to talk further with redT about potential development investment opportunities. Timing is everything. The first two investment opportunities in 2022 that were available to me were on syndicated, completely passive investments. One, a 52-unit townhome build in Aurora, and the other, a 5-unit townhome build in Denver. These were opportunities to earn high-teen returns, participate as a limited venture partner, and learn more about the overall development process.

Soon enough, the opportunity arose to be the sole developer of a project. I purchased infill land in an LLC via a hard money loan from Pine Financial and contracted with redT to build a 5-unit townhome in Denver. This opportunity enabled me to learn more about the end-to-end development process by ultimately being responsible for the final outcome. This includes the risk as well as financial liability undertaken with the higher level of loan this work requires. As of this writing, I now own four of these infill projects with a total of 15 doors in various stages of development and sale, with expected returns from early 2024 through late 2025.

## 2024 Goals

This brings me to 2024 and beyond...continue investing! In all seriousness, my high-level strategy/hope is to continue to build a pipeline of development investment projects. I love being part of the creation and transformation process associated with building something new (have I mentioned that before?!). I remain optimistic about the undersupply in our market and like the idea of creating new infill supply.

Many variables could impact that, and I plan to monitor the local market, the overall economy, and geo-political situations.

Some specific goals:

- Participate more regularly in local industry events to build my RE network—at least 2 per month.

- Seek out new development opportunities.  The target is 6 doors at $100k/door profit per year, assuming some will hit as planned and some may not.

- Structure my investing entities to minimize the tax exposure from the ordinary investment income incurred from development investing.

- Learn more about raising money in case larger opportunities present themselves.

- Expand my reading list beyond technology leadership to include more real estate and finance topics.  Target at least 3 this year.

- Craft a more specific vision of what I would like my RE business to look like.

- Seek opportunities to help others by sharing investing knowledge, making connections, or helping with professional development.

I will be anxious to look back a year from now to see how I have progressed with these goals and how all of us in the investing community have performed with whatever changes we see in rates, inventory, prices, and transaction volumes.  That said, I always remain poised to course-correct should conditions dictate.

On a side note, I was recently made redundant from the technology company I worked for and am looking for opportunities in the real estate space to apply the skills and knowledge I have developed over the years.  I am open to doing something new, such as establishing a more formal investing entity, partnering on a real estate effort, or working with a real estate investing or development company. Please reach out if you have any suggestions.

As I wrap this up, I would like to formally thank Chris and Nathan for their guidance and support in the last couple of years. I have also met many others from whom I have learned a great deal, and I appreciate all the relationships I have built. If there is anything I can help you with or knowledge I can share, I am happy to connect. Good luck to all!

# Jeff White

## 2023 Review and 2024 Goals and Strategies

What an amazing year! I finally left my W2 job in Q4 2023 to pursue being a full-time investor/realtor and living my best life with my wife! It's so awesome, and I can't believe all that has happened in 6 years since I started my journey in 2017.

## Quick 2023 Highlights:

1.  Left W2 Job after working a W2 since 2006.

2.  I did NOT purchase another house hack since my first priority was leaving my W2 and having a healthy cushion of savings to step into my new passion of helping fellow house hackers.

3.  Hit over 90k in net rental income, which was my best year yet.

4.  Hit 144k in Gross Commissions as a realtor, also my best year as a realtor yet.

5.  I took the longest vacation trip I've ever been on (honeymoon #2).

Here are my 2024 goals to review with commentary.

## Goals for 2024

Real Estate Goals

Goal 1: Optimize 3 units in my portfolio

Due to inflation, three units are not fully optimized and aren't achieving their best returns.

**Property 1:** Switch market tenant who's below market rents and switch to a Section 8 tenant. The difference between market rents and Section 8 rents on this unit is over $600 per month, so it doesn't make sense to continue to rent to market tenants when I'm leaving money on the table with Section 8.

**Property 2**: Switch a rent by room unit with 3 people, to a 4 bedroom Section 8 tenant. My goal is to downsize the number of tenants in my portfolio but not the rental income. I would add another bedroom to the property and downsize from three separate tenants to one Section 8 tenant.

**Property 3**: Switch a rent by room house to another sober living home. Instead of renting to 7 separate rent by room tenants, I would rent to one tenant who would operate the sober living home. End result, less maintenance by renting to one operator instead of trying to handle seven different leases for individual rooms.

Goal 2: Purchase the Ultimate 8th House Hack

My lender, Joe Massey, told me years ago that the record for the most number of house hack/nomad properties was 7 properties, and I told him at that time, half joking and half serious, that I would hit 8 properties to be the gold standard investor, and now, in 2024, I have that opportunity to hit that record. I'm excited to be able to accomplish hacking 8 properties after only starting my journey 7 years ago!

For number #8, I'm looking for a 2-4 unit property or a house with ADU in the Denver metro area. My wife and I plan on living in one unit and renting out the others or living in the ADU. For this one, the goal is simple: 10% cash on cash return, which is way above the average deal in the Denver metro market.

Goal 3: Stabilize All Properties with Self-Management and Software

Right now, I am transitioning all the property management in-house to my wife. She will be the main point of contact for contractors, tenant screening, ongoing maintenance, repairs, and exceptional service and support for all the tenants.

Also, we are switching from using old-school Excel spreadsheets to a software system called Hemlane, which automates accounting, makes lease tracking more efficient, and keeps property information organized.

It is interesting to look back at my goals and see how much I wanted property management. However, with good self-management and the right systems in place, the amount of work can be manageable so that it doesn't interfere with daily activities. I will consider hiring a property manager again someday, but not today.

**Goal 4:** Hit 120k in net rental income

By optimizing the 3 units previously mentioned, I'm likely to earn over 10k in net rental income per month.

Personal Goals

**Goal 1:** Travel at least once a month to a new city or country

My wife and I love each other's company, and I don't want to take this newfound time/money freedom to explore the world for granted. I want to take advantage of being a 1099 contractor and take spontaneous trips and time off with my wife to enjoy the outdoors, food, and each other.

**Goal 2:** Fitness

I'd like to improve my overall health and well-being. I'm committing to a fitness routine by going to the gym at least three times a week.

Business Goals:

**Goal 1:** Grow Realtor Business to a Higher Level

I want to focus on being the best house hacker/investor-friendly agent out there that helps all types of people accomplish their financial goals by utilizing creative strategies to achieve better-than-average returns.

Last year, I achieved great success as a part-time realtor for ten months of the year, hitting my highest numbers ever at 144k, and this year, I want to help twice as many people start and continue their financial independence journey as a full-timer in 2024.

Goal 2: Ultimate Guide to House Hacking v2

I'm helping to rewrite the Ultimate Guide to House Hacking since a lot has changed since we wrote it back in 2020. For one, rates aren't 3% anymore, so the strategies have evolved, too. However, the book is coming in 2024.

## Other Thoughts

Financial freedom and independence are journeys that demand patience, commitment, and discipline. We are proof that achieving financial freedom is within reach for anyone willing to take the necessary steps. I'm so grateful that this newfound freedom has granted my wife and me the flexibility to enjoy a more secure and fulfilling life—it's amazing! I hope to inspire and empower individuals to achieve their goals by openly sharing my journey. Together, we can build a stronger and more economically resilient community.

Bring on 2024, and let us all crush it together!

# Jim Tiernan

I am a buy-and-hold investor. I also invest in real estate notes. I quit my corporate job in 2023 after 25 years. I live in Denver, love to travel and will probably look for a part time job in real estate at some point. I am always looking for more rentals and real estate notes.

Connect with Jim at (303)-828-8109 or Jim@GrizzlyHomeBuyers.com or www.GrizzlyHomeBuyers.com, www.GrizzlyRentalSolutions.com.

## About My Strategy

While I have been primarily a buy-and-hold investor since 2008, I have been learning more about mortgage notes. The banks have learned that you don't have to OWN the property to make money from it. I sold one of my Chicago suburban rentals on a note in July 2022. So far, so good. It increased my cash flow by 72%, and I no longer need to worry about management, maintenance, taxes, insurance, and vacancies. I had owned the property since 2013, and since the Chicago population and prices were relatively flat, I was ok with selling this property on a note as a learning experience. I still have an underlying mortgage with a bank. My buyer pays me, I pay my bank and keep the difference. It's true; I no longer own the property, but I'm getting more cash flow. Real estate investors usually don't understand why people own notes, and note investors don't understand why people own rentals. I get it. So, the bottom line going forward is that I'm looking for properties (long-term appreciation, tax benefits) AND notes (more cash flow, fewer headaches). Ideally, I look for notes on properties owned by long-term landlords who want out of the rental game. If those long-time landlords don't want another rental and sell for cash, they will usually get killed in taxes. A 1031 exchange won't help them as they want to avoid another rental. But if they sell on an installment sale, they can keep some cash flow and spread that tax over many years.

I'd also like to dip my toes into investing in syndications (via the Property Llama crew?) and international real estate. Just as Colorado isn't the only state to invest in, the U.S. isn't the only country to invest in. Life is short, so I want to explore that option. I have Irish citizenship and may live at least part-time overseas at some point. Who knows, maybe I will get a 3rd passport somewhere on the beach. I write this as it is 8 below zero, and I am leaving to play hockey. I know it is warmer somewhere, and I need to work on my tan.

## My Current Portfolio

- 2 condos owned with my sister in Lakewood.

- 1 SFR in suburban Chicago with long-time Sec 8 renter - currently For Sale.

- 1 SFR Note in suburban Chicago (see About My Strategy).

- 33% of a 4-unit rehab in Pueblo - over time and over budget - keep or sell it?

- 33% of an SFR in Colorado Springs - lot zoned multi-family, but For Sale to cover Pueblo rehab above.

- 50% of a second SFR in Colorado Springs - zoned multi-family. The plan is to build 12 townhomes.

## 2024 Real Estate Goals

- The One Thing: Increase Net Operating Income on rentals by 15%. NOI is future cash flow. I will need to add a rental or real estate note.

- Increase Cash Flow on rentals by 15%.

- Reduce Bad Debt by 60% (I have HELOC in the Bad Debt category, also a credit card).

- Create 2 wrap mortgages (buy on seller financing, sell on seller financing), which will generate $1000 a month in cash flow.

- Sell Suburban rental in Chicago - 1031 (or not) into something in Colorado or pay tax and put it into a syndication.

- Sell first SFR zoned for multi-family in Colorado Springs.

- Finish Pueblo rehab.  Decide whether to rent, refinance and keep, or sell it.

- Finish building plans and get construction financing for 12 townhome projects in Colorado Springs.

- Set up and fund SDIRA with 401K money.

- Place 40% of SDIRA funds into Real Estate Syndications.

- Place 60% of SDIRA into Real Estate Notes.

- Get accredited investor status whenever the government creates an accredited investor test.

- Reorganize Net Worth:

    - 10% of Net Worth in Cash/Insurance (currently 12%).

    - 10% of Net Worth in precious metals (currently 8%; some people like stocks or crypto, I don't).

    - 55% of Net Worth in Domestic Real Estate (currently 80%).

    - 10% of Net Worth in International Real Estate (currently 0%).

    - 7.5% of Net Worth in Real Estate Notes (currently 0%).

    - 7.5% of Net Worth in Real Estate Syndications (currently 0%).

## 2024 Personal Goals

- Spend 1 day a month outdoors doing something fun—camping, Fishing, Golfing, Hiking, Snowboarding, or Snowshoeing.  I need to remember why I moved to Colorado in the first place!

- Exercise - 4 times a week.  3 cardio workouts (hockey, bike, treadmill) and 1 day lifting weights.

- Domestic Travel - 14 days.

- International Travel - 14 days (I spent all of July 2022 in Scandinavia; I can get used to that).

- Visit 1 new country every year - 18 visited at last count.

- Read 1 Non-Real Estate Book every quarter.  Wait, there are NON-real Estate books?

# Joey Schneider

On August 31st, 2022, I was laid off from my corporate 9-5 job. This was the third time I was laid off in the pharmaceutical industry during my 17-year career.

Hello. My name is Joey Schneider, and I'm here to share my story alongside my wife, Meredith. Allow me to paint a picture of who I am for those who haven't met me.

Following my college years, I spent some time in the rental car industry in Houston, TX, while my wife pursued her doctorate in medical school. She was training to be an eye care physician while I was still trying to figure out life after graduating from Texas Tech University with two degrees. After a couple of years in the rental car agency and rapidly progressing to leadership, I leaped into the dynamic pharmaceutical industry. Let the fun begin!

My initial foray into the pharma industry was as a sales professional at a small company. I achieved consecutive president's club honors only to leave that company after two years so my wife could pursue a partnership at a medical practice in Lubbock, TX, after graduating. I felt like I hit a home run by landing another pharma sales position with a massive global pharmaceutical company...two years later, I was laid off for the first time in my short career after posting a ranking of seventh best sales professional in the company. It didn't make sense to me, but I landed a similar role at another global pharmaceutical giant.

After six years with the second company, I advanced into leadership. During this time in Lubbock, TX, Meredith and I were enamored with new construction and the entire renovation process of rehabbing homes. Hence, our love for Fix and Flips was born...and the side hustle began.

Meredith was one of two partners in a medical practice in Lubbock, TX, for four years until she took over the practice and expanded it to two locations. Over the years, she improved the two practices to the point where she needed to hire other physicians to work for her to keep scaling. Around this time, I was promoted to leadership, and my company proposed a move to Colorado. As a couple, we decided that Colorado was where our adventure would continue, so Meredith sold her two practices to a group of doctors, and we turned the page to start our new adventures in Colorado.

During our time in Colorado, we witnessed a flourishing passion for real estate investing. We continued the side hustle and took part in a new construction project. For a few years, we wanted to build up our portfolio, so we purchased a single-family rental property in Central Florida. We did this by leveraging my 401k and transferring it into a self-directed IRA. This avenue for investing was an art that needs to be spoken of more often!

We bought in a booming area and plan to hold it for a few more years and make a handsome profit upon exit. After significant research prior to that purchase, we understood the direction that appreciation was headed in the real estate market. We also employed the services of a stellar property manager to handle the day-to-day. This freed up our time to continue with our 9-5's. The day will soon come when we will be able to cash out on that project!

Wanting to continue to expand our portfolio, we wanted rental property outside of the self-directed IRA so that we could start building our passive income. For this reason, we purchased duplexes in West Texas, where we lived for many years. We did this by taking a HELOC out on our current home, which had appreciated exponentially over a few short years in Colorado. This HELOC allowed us to fund our down payments for the duplexes and leverage financing for the remainder. The returns on the duplex far exceeded the interest rate on the HELOC, and we were able to generate some nice passive income. We employed the services of a property manager on these doors as we still had our day jobs.

During all this time, Meredith continued her work as an eye care physician and worked at multiple eye care practices in Denver and the mountains. I, too, continued in my leadership position until I was laid off a second time after spending nearly a decade at this third pharma company. This is when I realized that no matter how much effort I put into a company, how well I performed, or how much of an impact I had on the company's growth or the people, corporate America didn't care. I was let go without much thought to them, and it revealed the harsh truth about corporate America's indifference. On the flip side, I was thrilled to have the side hustle of Fix and Flips, single-family and multifamily rental properties.

Disheartened, I felt like I was in a place where I needed to push on and get another leadership position in Pharma. Trust me, as I write this, it sounds crazy in hindsight, but I did it anyway. While at this fourth company, I quickly accelerated my career by winning multiple awards, including the coveted Presidents Club award as a leader. Once again, I was attributing to the growth of the company and many sales professionals in a super gratifying way!

During my time at this company, my workload was significant. Meredith continued working as an eye care physician and shared a similar workload. We sacrificed our weekends, nights, and free time to continue our real estate investing side hustle. We didn't want the side hustle to stay the same; we wanted to grow it and scale it to something bigger. At this pivotal moment, Trinity Peak Partners, our investment company, was born.

My work colleague for many years, Nick Elder, became a close friend to Meredith and me in the early years in Colorado. Nick is also an author in this book and earlier versions as well. We all connected on a level that was unmatched in my mind. All three of us shared one common interest, and it was an important one: REAL ESTATE. We all had the passion, knowledge, and tenacity to get Trinity Peak

Partners off the ground and off to the races! So, the three of us became business partners and haven't looked back!

Nick and I worked together at two pharmaceutical companies, and it just so happens that he and I were together when we got laid off for the last time. Back to the beginning of my chapter, it was August 31st, 2022. Both Nick and I decided not to go back to the corporate world. Regarding Meredith's thoughts... she was in FULL support of me not returning to Pharma. Instead, she encouraged me to put all my efforts into Trinity Peak Partners. There aren't words to describe the support I received from Meredith. This type of support from a spouse is critical, so we were on the same page moving forward in the world of real estate investing.

Collectively, as a team at Trinity Peak Partners, we had rental properties in Colorado, Florida, and Texas and many fix-and-flip projects under our belts. It's time to scale!

In 2023, we bought and sold properties in Colorado, acquired fix-and-flips in three states, performed rehab and construction on seven properties, and, last but not least, acquired an apartment complex in NW Arkansas. We had an incredible year of building relationships, building teams, and working flawlessly and effortlessly as a team.

I was CEO, Meredith was CFO, and Nick was COO. Together, titles didn't matter, but succeeding did! We all figured out very quickly what our strengths and opportunities were. We relied on each other to fill the gaps, persevere, and push forward to scale Trinity Peak Partners.

The relationships we built along the way were the most valuable attributes we accomplished. Our mission was to build relationships, bring value, and help investors generate passive income and grow their wealth. We are grateful beyond words to the teams, GCs, wholesalers, agents, brokers, property managers, and investors we have met along the way. Lifelong relationships were gained, and we are all helping each other succeed in more ways than one.

Our goals in 2023 were to purchase three fix-and-flips/BRRRRs, build teams in two geographical areas, grow our real estate investing network, self-educate, and purchase one apartment complex. Needless to say, we crushed those goals! Thankful is not a strong enough word for how the three of us feel about our accomplishments in 2023. At the same time, we know we are capable of more!

We recently had our Trinity Peak Partners 2024 "Goal Sesh" at the beginning of January. Our goals as a company are quite ambitious for this coming year. We have targets to acquire at least 20 fix-and-flips/BRRRRs and three apartment complexes. We have NEVER been this ostentatious with our goals...and I LOVE IT!

Investing in real estate has been more fulfilling than Meredith and I ever imagined. We work hard and play even harder. We have FUN and have the ability to work from anywhere. The geographical freedom this career provides is unreal. The financial freedom part of this role is very near in the distance...and I can see it. Years ago, the thought of financial and time freedom was not even in the picture. It's surreal to see how fast things can change when you decide to put in the effort and work relentlessly to make it happen.

With the efforts made in 2023 and the goals we have in place for 2024, Meredith has recently decided to go ALL-IN on Trinity Peak Partners as well! This will allow us to pursue more opportunities, get more done, and scale our investment company. I couldn't be more excited to work alongside her in this chapter of our lives. Let the adventure continue!

My advice if anyone wants it...stop making excuses. The life that you want is out there. It requires effort, perseverance, consistency, tenacity, and a positive growth mindset. I can't express enough how important a person's mindset is. Take some time to evaluate yourself and the people you surround yourself with. Read and listen to podcasts and books that help you grow into the person you want to be. Take healthy risks, step outside your comfort zone, challenge your fears, block out the naysayers, and go after your dreams. You CAN do it!

Meredith and I dream of financial, geographical, and time freedom. What's yours? Are you willing to sacrifice? Are you willing to work hard to get there? Are you willing to continuously learn? Are you willing to fail so you can learn from your mistakes and grow because of them? Ask yourself, what's stopping me? Figure out what that is, then eliminate it.

I couldn't be more excited to build even more genuine relationships, help others get into the real estate investing game, help others build their passive income, and mentor those who want to get started. If I haven't met you yet, I look forward to meeting YOU!

Follow Trinity Peak Partners on LinkedIn, Facebook, and Instagram to follow our projects. Just search the company name. Our Instagram is @trinitypeakpartners.

To learn more about Meredith and me, follow us on LinkedIn. Again, just give our names a search!

My personal Instagram is @joey.colorado.4r. Here, you'll find photos that follow our adventures in life!

Email: joey@trinitypeakpartners.com, meredith@trinitypeakpartners.com

Phone: 832-971-3036

# Kelly Mahana

Before I Dive In, I want to give a huge thank you to Chris Lopez for extending this invitation to me and having me as a guest on his podcast. I would also like to thank Jeff White for our unlikely friendship and your support of my wife and me since meeting you almost two years ago. Bre, my beautiful wife, you're my best friend and biggest supporter; I Love you.

## My Journey

I want to share my journey from generational poverty and gang involvement to my aspirations as an investor.

At the age of 10, I found myself caught up in a cycle of poverty and violence that seemed inescapable. The streets became my home, and I became entangled in the world of gangs. This path led me down a destructive road, eventually landing me in the juvenile justice system.

However, my life took a dramatic turn when, just three months after being released from juvenile prison, I found myself facing another legal battle. As a teenager, I was sentenced to an unimaginable 60 years in prison. The weight of that sentence felt insurmountable, and it seemed like my life was over.

Through the grace of God and the guidance of a jailhouse lawyer, I was able to navigate the legal system and have my sentence reduced by 40 years. After serving 13 years behind bars, I was finally released back into society.

This experience has shaped my perspective on life and ignited a burning desire within me to break free from the chains of my past. I realized I had been given a second chance and was determined to make the most of it.

## My Path Forward

I understand that building wealth is about accumulating money and creating opportunities for myself and others. Through strategic investments, I aim to break the cycle of poverty that has plagued my family for generations.

My investing goals for 2024 reflect my determination to create a better future for myself and my family. By leveraging my experiences and knowledge, I am committed to building a portfolio that will provide long-term financial security and open doors for others who have faced similar struggles.

In sharing my story and investing goals, I hope to inspire others who have faced adversity to believe in their potential and realize that it is never too late to rewrite their own narrative. Together, we can break free from the limitations of our past and create a brighter future filled with hope, success, and prosperity.

In 2023, I made a significant career transition, moving from working two full-time jobs to focusing solely on my business, Authentic Recovery Homes. Throughout the year, I expanded my business from one residence to four, all of which are currently rented out. This growth has allowed me to establish a stable foundation for my investment goals in 2024.

## My 2024 Goals

For the upcoming year, my primary goal is to purchase two properties. The first property will be a 2-4 unit building, where my wife and I will live in one unit and lease out the others to Section 8 tenants. This approach will not only provide us with a place to live but will also allow us to lower our monthly expenses.

The second property we plan to acquire will be a single-family home with an ADU (Accessory Dwelling Unit). We intend to move into the ADU and utilize the main house as a Sober Living Home, expanding our business further. This strategic move will allow us to exit one of our current locations as the lease expires, reducing expenses and increasing our cash flow.

In addition to real estate investments, I aim to make significant contributions to my dividend portfolio. With the additional revenue streams from the sober living home, I will have more capital available to invest in dividend-paying stocks. This will help diversify my investment portfolio and generate passive income over time.

Lastly, I plan to focus on networking and building relationships in 2024. By establishing strong connections within the sober living community and related industries, I aim to minimize vacancies in our homes. This proactive approach will ensure a steady stream of participants and further enhance the financial stability of our business.

Overall, my investing goals for 2024 revolve around creating a real estate portfolio of two properties, each with a different strategy, increasing passive income through dividends, and strengthening my business through networking and relationship building. With careful planning and execution, I am confident that I can achieve these goals and continue to grow both personally and professionally.

# Ken Hobbick

I have been reading the annual guide to Colorado Real Estate Investing for the past 5 years and have routinely set yearly and quarterly goals; however, this will be the first year of merging these two areas of my life, contributing my own investing strategy in this year's edition.  Looking back over the years to try and begin to provide a brief synopsis, to sum up my approach, the best way I have been able to describe it is to be diversified—having more than one asset class while also being fluid enough, courageous enough, and a willingness to change and adapt your strategy to market conditions taking into account personal circumstances, networks, and abilities.

I hope that some people will benefit from this information.   Collaborating and sharing is one aspect of the real estate investing community that I find astonishing, as most investors have an abundance mindset and a willingness to share their knowledge and experiences with people who seek it out.  Personal finance is just that, "personal," what is right for me may not be right for someone else, which is equally true for real estate investing.  Through various stages in life and changing market conditions, I have made investments even 5 years ago that I would not do again in today's environment.   Being a lifelong learner through books, podcasts, and networking has resulted in applying various concepts learned over the years to fit different stages in life.

## Investment Strategy:  Get Started and Join an Investor Class

Balance is key, which holds true in life as well as investing.  It's far more of a journey than simple acts of sequential investments over time, but some foundational truths should be applied, the first of which I discovered and used early in life after reading... you guessed it: *Rich Dad Poor Dad*.  It starts with removing yourself from being an employee and trading time and hours of your life in return for money to the investor class or business class to generate passive income. The rest can be thought of as details of the plan to accomplish this.... Individual results will vary.

Early in my career, I worked as a Nuclear Medicine Technologist, which was very dependent on direct patient care and hands-on trading hours for time. I have done some consulting and contract work in nuclear medicine, but due to cost, the option to build a business in this area was best left to radiology practices and hospitals.

So, the next best option to owning a business was to join an investor class. The easiest way to get started was through 401k contributions via an employer. The most important part of this equation is that I got started and invested the maximum amounts early on, lived below my means, and invested the difference. Living below your means and having the ability to invest the difference is another foundational truth—if you get this one wrong, nothing else will make a difference. Interestingly, this was during the growth phase of the dot.com era, so funds were posting 80% returns. I was young and aggressive, and my strategy was to invest in these stocks (not seeing the writing on the wall) with balance and some diversification. Luckily, I did not invest everything into high-flying tech stocks. The first lesson learned when investing in stocks is to be prepared to lose a sizable portion of value.

Don't worry; I still had the advantage of time to recoup any losses, and I followed the mantra of the financial community to keep investing—dollar cost average and diversify your investments. Then, the 2008 financial crisis caused another significant drop in value. Looking back, I thought it would have been enough if I had diversified in different market sectors and had a good mix of bonds. However, how diversified can you be if you are invested only through Wall Street? One influential and revealing book was Tony Robbins's *Money Master the Game*. This well-researched book includes in-depth interviews with financial experts, such as Jack Bogel, creator of index funds, and how he ended up with more than 10,000 mutual funds, more than the number of underlying stocks of the companies that make up the mutual funds. Additionally, it highlights the famous one-million-dollar challenge from Warren Buffet to anyone in the hedge fund industry who could outperform the S&P 500 over a ten-year period starting in 2008, which Warren Buffet and the S&P had won versus any active investing hedge fund. The second lesson learned is to keep it simple and invest in Index funds.

I provide this brief overview because of an educated assumption that this describes most people's investment strategies through employers' 401k if they are fortunate enough to have one and have yet to realize what options are available to them.

I underwent a career change after the financial crisis, moving to radiology administration and eventually into IT project management for radiology PACS, for which I continued doing consulting/contract work. In 2012, we rented out our primary residence in Colorado to move across the country and realized the benefits real estate can provide.

Fast forwarding a few more years to 2015, we found ourselves with most of our net worth in 401k and wanting to start investing in SFR with a long-term buy-and-hold strategy. Another aspect of investing includes a mindset shift in your thinking to move from "I can't afford this" to "How can I afford this?". Despite this mindset shift, I found no good option to utilize 401k funds. Some of the options I considered included cashing out 401k with a 10% early withdrawal penalty and taxes... that was enough of a deal breaker. Option of 401k loans—this one sounds like a good option, and pay your 401k back with interest. Still, when you follow the logic of this approach, you take funds out of a tax-deferred IRA and then use your after-tax dollars via payroll to pay the loan back to your IRA, which eventually you will pay taxes on the proceeds and the 6% you paid your IRA to use your funds. Not to mention, if you leave your employer, you are required to pay the loan back. Self-directed IRA route- since the IRA is tax-deferred, you lose the advantage of applying the depreciation of the property. In addition, financing would require a non-recourse loan with up to 40% down payment and a higher interest rate than the same income property in your personal name. Your IRA can be taxed with UBIT (unrelated business income tax), which is applied to any portion of profits resulting from the use of financed debt. Lastly, you cannot personally use, benefit, or work on the property as this is characterized as a prohibited transaction. The penalty for committing a prohibited transaction in your IRA is the entire IRA is dissolved, and taxes are due. As a result, we invested in our first out-of-state rental the old-fashioned way, stopped contributing to 401k, and worked extra jobs to save for a down payment.

## Investment Strategy: Out of State Buy and Hold

We invested in two out-of-state properties in Indianapolis and Jacksonville, FL. Both properties were very similar; both were turn-key purchases at the price of $110k, cash flow negative while experiencing evictions of inherited tenants in the first 6 months of ownership, but did provide an opportunity to complete a 1031 exchange into SFR in Colorado Springs in 2021. (For a summary of this, you can listen to podcast #92 on Colorado Springs Real Estate Investing)

Initially, the investment strategy was a long-term buy-and-hold strategy; knowing these are mostly linear markets without high appreciation, it was a get-rich slow process with nominal appreciation. Looking back, one crucial consideration of these first income property investments was the price point, which was low enough to get started with a $25k down payment to start investing, and it was the best investment at the time, considering the market and our circumstances. Perhaps most importantly, it started the process and provided more options later in life for better investments.

Since it was a long-distance investment, we were at the mercy of property managers who could have managed the rentals better. Consequently, both properties had negative cash flow. I still operate on the assumption that no matter how good the property manager is, they will care less about your property than you do. There are always pros and cons to using property management companies, and one pro was the passivity of these investments, which I was thankful for when a pipe broke in one of the houses and caused a flood. I didn't have to deal with it, just the bill for water remediation. During this 3-4 year period of holding these properties, I was still intent on finding a better way to invest in real estate through 401k accounts.

## Investment Strategy: Self-Directed 401k and Multiple Income Streams

It was early 2017 when I ran across a podcast on Bigger Pockets episode #211, "Investing in out-of-state rentals and notes," with Bob Malecki about the advantages of note investing and comparing it with out-of-state rentals, which began an intense learning process and networking that ultimately lead to partnering with established note investors utilizing my 401k. The simplest explanation to note investing is stepping into the place of the bank. You purchase a bank-originated mortgage sold on the secondary market, in which case you are listed as a lien holder on the title of assignments, which is recorded at the county, along with the right of foreclosure to enforce mortgage payment. By far, most people will stay current with their mortgage. Still, some borrowers will inevitably experience something that causes a default, such as loss of job, sickness, or death in the family, in which case the bank will sell off the defaulted mortgage. This was when the inventory of defaulted mortgage notes was still being worked through from the financial crisis, even 10 years later. The ability to work with borrowers and iron out a loan modification to allow them to keep their homes and get back on their feet also presented an opportunity for investors.

There are commonalities between real estate investing and note investing. However, note investing has fewer classifications; it's either a performing loan or non-performing loan and 1$^{st}$ position lien or 2$^{nd}$ position lien. For example, it is possible to rehab a non-performing loan through a loan modification and make it a performing loan, which increases its value and can be sold to a passive investor interested in cash flow. Real estate has property managers, and note investors have loan servicers, such as FCI Services or Madison Management Services, who handle payments from borrowers, communications, licensing, and ensure regulations are followed.  On the other hand, note investing lacked any tax advantage, and it was not possible to use leverage to purchase mortgage notes, so this was an opportunity to join the 2% of the population who have a self-directed IRA and the ability to invest in alternative assets and to diversify away from Wall Street truly.

Once I moved to a self-directed IRA, it opened additional avenues for investing.  The list of restricted items established by the IRS that you cannot invest in with your traditional IRA is actually very small; it includes life insurance, unhedged short derivative positions, collectibles such as artwork, primary residence, and personal property... namely anything that benefits you or your direct descendants directly.  The financial industry and brokerage accounts limit your investment options in your 401k.  I was fortunate enough to find a self-directed IRA company founded by multi-generational attorneys who are also active real estate investors and provided a great foundation based on education and networking.

At this point, my self-directed IRA strategies have included investing in private placement entities, which would be an LLC set up specifically to partner with experienced note investors.  The critical component in this scenario is that your IRA (or yourself) is not actively involved in the operation of the LLC.  The second option for mortgage notes was to purchase mortgage notes directly in the name of your IRA account.  My strategy was to only do this for performing notes or partial notes due to the passive nature.  The loan servicers collect the payments, deduct their $20/month service fee, and send payment to your IRA.  The caveat to any investment made through your IRA is that all expenses related to the asset purchased must be paid through your IRA, which can become cumbersome over time.

It's worth mentioning that note investing involves considerable risk, and it is very much a buyer-beware market. I was fortunate enough to partner with experienced and established investors in the note space and learn first-hand. I highly recommend that if you are considering purchasing any notes, you find a trusted mentor who can help, as there can be land minds to avoid in terms of JV Partners, who have a list of judgments against them from past investors who lost their funds.

Opportunity is not without risks; note investing is a small niche market. The process and ability to purchase notes is one of the more challenging obstacles to overcome initially, although Paperstac.com has since been developed to help facilitate the process between buyers and sellers. It's also very much a "buyer beware" industry, and due diligence is entirely in the hands of the buyer. Case in point, I had a loan I was selling on Paperstac.com, and the potential buyer sent me a link to a story in the local paper with the headline "Firefighter responds to fire at his own house." It turns out it was the same house where I was selling a second lien mortgage without knowing about the fire. It all worked out, as the house was rebuilt, and nothing diminished the value of the 2nd mortgage, but it took me by surprise. Many loans were being sold by significant hedge funds that couldn't keep track of the current status of the properties, which presented both opportunities and risks. In one of the very few mortgage notes I encountered in Colorado, it was a 2nd lien mortgage for sale at 20% of the unpaid balance, but the property was also for sale and under contract, which effectively means the loan would be paid off at the sale of the house. We contacted the buyer, who agreed to sell the loan, and we agreed to wire the funds immediately, but it ended up being too late, and the sale of the property had already paid off the loan. If we had been a day earlier, we would have made around $15k on that transaction for simply recognizing the sale of the property.

## Investment Strategy: Know the Right Time to Pivot

Ultimately, over three years, I diversified my investment portfolio through note investing, and, in a way, it was similar to flipping and rehabbing houses, which provides opportunities to sell off some properties and then keep the best for your own portfolio. A similar strategy can be applied to mortgage notes, as I retained a few performing notes with payment amortization schedules ranging from 5 to 30 years. Performing notes are bought and sold based on yield, and since I was able to buy them at a discounted rate of a non-performing loan and work through a modification, it works out to be a 15-20% yield for the long-term future, which is another good match up for a 401k and long-term horizon. In the overall investment strategy, I consider these remarkably similar to bonds producing monthly payments and secured against real estate.

Even though there was an inventory of notes for sale from 2015 to 2018, it became increasingly more difficult to find sources of defaulted notes to buy, along with the time and expense to work out loan modifications because most loans being sold were located in judicial states. Compounded with risks moving into 2020 and the year of the COVID shutdown, I was determined to sell off the remaining non-performing loans and return my focus on buy and hold SFRs. I recall selling a non-performing loan in March of 2020 in St Louis, in which the borrower's income was from owning a bar and grill. I still wonder how that one worked out, but I consider myself fortunate to see the writing on the wall.

## Investment Strategy: Roth Conversion and Taxes

For the past 5 years, I have also focused on contributing and moving as many assets as possible to Roth IRAs. The advantage of a Roth IRA is significant because the earnings are allowed to grow, and then they can be withdrawn tax-free and not count towards your taxable income later in life. This is counterbalanced by the current laws restricting income and the amount you can contribute. However, currently, it is possible to convert IRA funds to Roth IRA without the income restriction encountered in the past. Still, the conversion is added to your taxable income during the year of conversion. It may be difficult to believe, but historically, we are at all-time low tax rates. I ran across a book called *Roth for the Rich* by Will Duffy, detailing the history of IRAs, taxes, and how to use IRAs and Roths to their full advantage. It's difficult to sign up to pay additional taxes each year, but I would evaluate how much extra I could afford to pay in taxes, convert that amount, and continue this over several years to lower the impact. It's eye-opening once you do the math and the long-term impact it can have.

## Investment Strategy: 1031 Exchange into Colorado Springs

Habituality tracking my net worth is something I do quarterly, along with monthly income and expenses. It makes it easy to determine what portions of your portfolio and investment strategies are doing well, what needs attention, and what could be done better. "Could do better" was an accurate summary of the out-of-state investments mentioned earlier; even with the advantage of time to recoup initial losses after evictions, they both still had negative cash flow overall. One of the advantages of real estate investing is appreciation over time, which can be very forgiving of mistakes, and both properties had acquired around $75k of equity, which could be transferred to Colorado via 1031 exchange. Having options and the ability to control the asset is something I find very appealing about real estate investing. Since both out-of-state properties were older and experienced higher-than-average maintenance and repairs, it was essential to trade up and find newer properties and better tenants. I also had enough of property managers and decided to self-manage the properties, which I continue to this day.

Since this was at a time of historic low-interest rates, I could simultaneously trade up with the first 1031 exchange from a $175k 3 bed, 2 bath house in Indianapolis to a $385k 4 bed, 3 bath house in Colorado Springs. I was also able to do a cash-out refinance on our primary residence, so I would have additional funds available for reserves and add a third property in Colorado Springs. The second 1031 exchange involved a $177k 3 bed, 2 bath house in Jacksonville to a $275k 3 bed, 2 bath new build townhouse in Colorado Springs. Due to time restrictions involved with the

1031 exchange, a new build would usually be ruled out, but Jenny Bayless found a new build that was 80% complete that fell out of contract.

One aspect of my real estate strategy is to be open to new strategies when they make sense. In 2021, I heard about medium-term rentals to increase the property's performance. I have a background in health care, and it was appealing to provide a furnished rental to traveling healthcare workers. Since then, I have learned that only about 50% of my medium-term tenants are healthcare travelers, and the others comprise families in between houses, traveling academics, and working nomads.

Since the 3 bedroom townhouse was initially purchased in southern Colorado Springs to be a long-term rental and was the furthest away to self-manage a medium-term rental, I converted this to a long-term rental. I found the third property, in northern Colorado Springs, had an ideal location, and that was the one for the medium-term rental.

Your strategy can change once you have multiple properties and view them as a portfolio to evaluate their overall performance. I have changed the long-term buy-and-hold SFR strategy to include two long-term rentals and one medium-term rental. I'm not interested in accumulating as many properties as possible; it's more important to optimize the properties, maintain proper reserves, and be ready for the next opportunity when it presents itself. Another consideration I include is how much of my time and effort is required and what kind of work-life balance I am to achieve.

My overall investing strategy includes stocks/bonds in IRA, Roth IRA in traditional brokerage accounts such as Charles Schwab and Fidelity, self-directed IRA/Roth, and a small portfolio of income properties. Life has a way of building upon itself in terms of both opportunities and experiences. I found as time passes and I get closer to retirement age, the less the volatility and unpredictability of the stock market appeals to me, and essentially, the majority of the funds still invested in average

401k stock employer plans are there because I can't move them out until we stop working for these employers.

## Investment Strategy: Revisit Passive Self-Directed 401k Investing

In 2022, I did a career shift and left a long-time employer to begin IT project management consulting and gained access to additional 401k funds that could be moved to self-directed.   In 2022 and 2023, I incorporated more self-directed investments into alternative assets, this time in apartments and apartment funds. Having made previous investments through self-directed IRAs, I was comfortable with the added due diligence, process, and paperwork involved, as it is much more involved than just clicking the buy/sell button on your traditional IRA portal.  It made sense to include in my current portfolio being passive and having a 3–5-year time horizon, which also helps balance decisions as this portion of my investments are set, and likely to have a higher IRR than stocks/bonds and be able to leverage the value of experienced operators in multi-family space.  At times, Wall Street seems to offer no safe place for investments; it's just a fact that you will lose money occasionally; it's only a matter of how much and how often.

Market changes in 2023 produced high interest rates, which relegated most real estate investments to either be cash flow negative or require a larger percent down payment to make them cash flow, which is not the ideal situation.  These challenges can also produce opportunities when considering other investment strategies to optimize the performance of the properties.  This is when I first heard of the rent-by-room investment strategy, which I initially placed in the "additional work" category and may not be suitable for my "lifestyle right now" category.  Rent by room can significantly increase rents collected, but you have also increased the amount of work involved in managing the property with additional tenants, leases, turnover, cleaning, and maintenance, as well as ongoing operations of the property... not to mention the experience of successfully implementing this strategy.

After hearing about this strategy on Colorado Real Estate investing podcasts, I reached out for more information about this strategy and a potential partnership to work together. At this point, my experience of using self-directed 401k and past experiences with partnerships and JV agreements presented some opportunities, as it's possible to invest in LLCs as a private placement entity, but you will also need a trusted partner to manage the LLC. In this case, someone who has already used this strategy can find properties and maximize the rooms for rent. Another aspect to consider was the current lending options, as DSCR loans can be made to an LLC with 20% down compared to non-recourse loans requiring 40% down if made to an IRA directly. This provided a way to use 401k funds passively to invest directly into real estate and provide funding and partnership to other real estate investors.

The property, which was a 3200 sq ft 3 bed, 3 bath house with a partially finished basement at the time of purchase, was turned into a 6 bed, 4 bath house to optimize the rent-by-room model. This can also be combined with a medium-term rental strategy, with the basement built as a studio apartment with a separate entrance. As with most real estate investments, this will be evaluated on a long-term basis.

## 2024 Goals

Professional Goals-

- Continue working in IT Project Management on a contractual consulting basis, maintaining a healthy work-life balance.
- Continuing education and adding industry certification.
- Take advantage of being able to work remotely and take a working vacation on reduced working hours.

Investing Goals – 401k

- Complete a Roth Conversion on $25k.

- Increase IRA contributions to 15% of income.

- Max contributions to Roth accounts.

## Real Estate Goals

- Optimize current portfolio maintaining a high occupancy rate for medium-term rental and retain the current tenants in long-term rentals.

- Evaluate the option of finishing the basement in SFR – to either increase living space and rent or build a separate entrance and make a 1 bedroom studio apartment for medium-term rental.

- Maintain 6 months of reserves in rental property accounts.

## Personal Growth-Family Goals

- Volunteer more both individually and as a family.

- Support and financially educate teen daughters moving to independence and into college.

- Enjoy more travel with my wife and family.

- Monthly dates to review finances with my wife.

## Fitness Goals

- Workout 6 days a week, maintain healthy weight, and diet.

- Increase Hiking and Biking- 10 new hikes to explore Colorado.

- Hike a 14er this year since we didn't make it last year.

- Purchase at-home gym.

## About My Strategy

I often find it difficult to categorize exactly what my real estate investment strategy is because it has changed so significantly over time. This being my first submission, I went into greater historical detail in the hope that some readers can relate to my experiences and others can take some aspects they find helpful and implement them in their own situations. Seasons in your life change along with the market and available opportunities; I have never considered investing a right or wrong decision, but what is right for you and your current circumstances and take advantage of what you can. The most important part of the equation is to recognize a good opportunity when it comes.

Ken Hobbick is a diversified Real Estate investor who utilizes buy-and-hold long-term real estate and medium-term rental strategies. He is a former long-distance/out-of-state investor and a lifelong learner who focuses on optimizing the use of 401ks, self-directed IRAs, and Roth IRAs into alternative investments and more passive real estate investments.

Connect with Ken at khobbick@gmail.com

# Laura Pilcher

Laura Pilcher is an investor-friendly real estate agent with the New Era Group who helps clients buy, sell, and invest in real estate in the Denver Metro Area and the High Rockies of Colorado. She and her husband develop homes in the mountains, and you can follow them @100kCabin on Instagram or 100kcabin.com.

Connect with Laura at (303) 589-4028 or LauraPilcher@mynewera.com or https://mynewera.com/laura-pilcher/.

## About My Strategy – Survive and Scale!

2023 was all about pivoting. I am a relatively new investor, and I still get that sense of panic when everything doesn't happen the way you expect. What we learned in 2023 is that you can't control the market, so you have to be flexible in your investment strategy. For us, that meant selling the second cabin we built...even when I publicly stated in last year's guide that I would never sell another property we built! Never say never. For those of you who didn't read the 2023 guide, I got into real estate investing in 2015 when I bought an acre of land in the Colorado Rockies for $10k, then built an affordable cabin in Fairplay to avoid spending a small fortune every time I took my family skiing in Breckenridge. We built an 1,800 square foot modern mountain cabin for $160k. Pretty awesome. The bonus silver lining was we also made a tidy little income by short-term renting the cabin. Then Covid hit, and the STR market tanked, we got scared, and we sold our cabin for a little under $400k—150% profit - boom.

That felt good until the STR market rebounded, and we thought we had made a huge mistake in selling. We decided to build another cabin. In 2022, we completed our second mountain build, which was 2,500 square feet and cost us $277k to build. We tried renting it, but despite a healthy demand in the Fairplay area where we built, there were significantly more short-term rentals to choose from in the area, creating a saturated market. This resulted in renters wanting lower prices. We realized that this second build was not hitting the mark for us because of the combination of a higher cost to build, higher mortgage, and lower cash flow. We decided to pivot away from the STR strategy and sell the property. We sold it for $705k, resulting in a 154% profit.

Hooray! We made $428,000!!! That's exciting, right? Well, yes, but we got stuck with an ugly tax bill once again. We were smart enough to keep what we needed aside and pay our estimated taxes on time, but we still felt like we hadn't quite figured out the right strategy for us. After all was said and done, we paid off some debts, put some money in stocks, and forged ahead with our plans for our Granby new build. One great highlight was that simultaneously, we were able to convert our primary home into a long-term rental and purchase a new primary. Let me be clear—it was a stretch. It felt uncomfortable, but we had it rented within a day, and that extra $1500 monthly cash flow has been wonderful. We know this home will be an excellent long-term investment, so having someone else pay this off for us is fantastic.

Our new home is what I like to call a live-in flip. We are going to stay in it for 2 years to avoid short-term capital gains while adding value. It is a 4 bedroom, 3.5 bathroom, 3,800 square foot home with a ⅓ acre yard that we fell in love with. The home felt very 90s, so we updated it to be a more modern farmhouse style and are adding a full bathroom and closet to the basement to create a mother-in-law suite. There was already a great kitchen and living space in the basement and a bedroom with an egress window, so these last elements were needed to make it a mother-in-law suite. We believe this, along with the cosmetic updates we made, should really add value for resell. We hope to make approximately a $230k profit that we can apply to our next home, which we hope will be our forever home—or, at least, our home until our kids are grown.

That means in 2024, we are house hunting in Denver! It will be interesting to see what the market brings. We hope to sell our home in June and find a new home by the end of the summer.  If the real estate gods are smiling on us, we may even be able to sell our Granby build by the end of summer, too.  Then, we'll be looking for a couple of properties to 1031 exchange to avoid those blasted capital gains, and it will be time to let the scaling begin!

## 2023 Goals, Results, and Lessons Learned

These were my 2023 goals:

- Achieving a cash flow of $3-4k/month from the new Fairplay cabin.  DIDN'T HAPPEN, SO PIVOTED AND SOLD FOR A 154% PROFIT!

- Getting our ducks in a row financially to scale our business.  STILL WORKING ON THIS!

- Possibly buying a new lot of land in Granby.  THIS IS SOMETHING WE WILL CONSIDER AFTER SELLING OUR NEW BUILD IN GRANBY.

- Starting on our Granby new build - the goal is to spend no more than $500k to build and achieve a monthly cash flow of $5-7k by 2024.  BUDGET IS CURRENTLY MORE LIKE $600K, BUT THE BIG NEWS HERE IS WE ARE BUILDING TO SELL INSTEAD OF TRYING TO RENT IT FIRST.  THEN GOING TO 1031 EXCHANGE INTO 2 OR MORE PROPERTIES.

- Identifying 1 new Denver metro area SFH to invest in and long-term rent. The goal is to have 2 Denver metro area SFH to hold onto as long-term investments.  1 DOWN, 1 TO GO.  WE MAY PUT A DOWN PAYMENT ON A LTR IN TOWN WHEN WE 1031 EXCHANGE.

- Not go crazy or bankrupt!!  Just jokes...but seriously.  WE GOT REAL CLOSE. WHEN THE FAIRPLAY CABIN WAS NOT CASH-FLOWING AS WE IMAGINED, WE STARTED TO PANIC A BIT. THANKFULLY, WE SOLD IT, AND THE SALE WENT SO WELL, BUT WE LIVED ON THE EDGE THERE FOR A WHILE.  SOMEONE RECENTLY TOLD ME LIVING ON THE EDGE IS WHERE REAL CHANGE HAPPENS, AND I HAVE TO AGREE.

- Make even more connections with the Colorado RE investing community! THIS IS DEFINITELY A 2024 GOAL - I HAVE NOT BEEN ABLE TO MAKE AS MANY CONNECTIONS THIS YEAR AS I WOULD HAVE LIKED. CARVING OUT TIME FOR THIS IS IMPORTANT WORK. AND FUN!

## 2024 Goals

- 1031 exchange our new build in Granby (projected value is $1.3M, build cost approx. $600k) into two STRs, and possibly one LTR.

- Sell current primary after 2 year hold period and buy new primary!

- Achieve a $7,500 monthly cash flow from 2 STRs and 2 LTRs.

- Pick up another lot of land in the mountains and start shopping for some multifamily opportunities.

- The long-term goal is to achieve $15-19k monthly cash flow by 2028, and we will achieve that by SCALING. 2024 will be all about scaling.

# Matt Amundson

Matt Amundson has been a flipper and buy-and-hold investor in single-family homes in the Denver area since 2007. In 2018, he branched out into syndicating deals in Texas with partners and is now transitioning his buy-and-hold rentals into passive RE investments in multiple asset classes. A licensed agent with Your Castle Realty and an Investor Relations Specialist with Property Llama Capital, he loves talking deals with other investors and finding ways to help them achieve their investing goals.

Connect with Matt at (303)-941-0699 or matt.amundson@propertyllama.com

## About My Strategy

My strategy has undergone a fairly major transformation in the past year and a half, which I'll get to, but since this is my first chapter for this book, I'll give a brief history. I was able to buy our first home in 2005 and started saving up some cash, studying, and learning as much as I could. I was finally ready to start my investing career in 2007. Newly married and planning on starting a family, I knew I needed more income than I could make as a freelance musician, and I had always wanted to pursue RE investing. Starting out, I was flipping houses, trying to turn a small pile of cash into a larger one. Then I got stuck trying to flip my 5th house when this first-time home buyer tax credit, which supported a faltering housing market, ended. I was stuck with a flip when the market died. Luckily, I was able to do a cash-out refi and buy two more as rentals. If I was going to be stuck with one rental with no leverage, it was clear that leveraging that and two other houses was the best option. Time passed, and our second child was born. Then, in 2013, the appreciation grew to allow the purchase of another rental property in Aurora via cash-out refi. That was the base that I leaned on for many years. I thought I would keep my Denver rentals forever, thinking I would eventually split the portfolio among my two children.

I would flip the occasional house here and there when great deals arose. I was happy playing music and raising my kids, and we were comfortable with the lifestyle and stability that our rentals provided us. When the kids were both of school age, I decided it was time to get after the investing/business side of things so I could hit my financial freedom goals when my kids left the nest. I harvested more equity in 2018 and started syndicating deals with my friend and partner, Chris Lawhead. We did deals in CO and Texas and learned that out-of-state investing has many unforeseen challenges. Building up to a portfolio of 30 doors sounded cool, but it didn't provide the returns and lifestyle I was after. Working that hard and not quite crushing it as we had intended left me wondering what direction to take next.

**Here is the big shift that started taking place**. As an accredited investor, one has more options than someone with a small pile of cash, so I started looking into those options as a passive investor. I also utilized the Property Llama software, attended a portfolio analysis mastermind, and started looking at my trapped equity in a new light. Like so many of you, I have always benefited from the education and guidance of our wonderful community of investors, mainly Charles Roberts and Lon Welsh from Your Castle. My rentals had capped out on their growth potential, and though their cash flow was pretty decent, it was clear to me that the equity needed to be redeployed. Looking for good returns with less time to find and run deals, I decided to go into passive investments. There was much to learn about vetting sponsors and choosing the right investments for my long-term goals. There was also a lot of tax prep that I worked on very closely with my CPA to understand the tax implications of those moves and not overextend myself. I am very excited about this new path forward in my investing strategy.

## How I Started to Implement the Shift:

- I started my ladder approach into passive investments with some available cash in 2022.

- I sold two properties in the spring of 2023 to reinvest. I looked to double my overall returns on the equity in those properties. I was able to offset more than half of my tax burden by buying into funds that offered high levels of depreciation. Accelerated depreciation, through the use of cost segregation studies, is an efficient tax-delaying strategy like a 1031 exchange. I had another $100k to invest last year from my paper losses through the depreciation. When those funds mature, I will look at what legal tax avoidance strategies are available or just pay the $100k I deferred this year - interest free! - to Uncle Sam.

## My Plan for 2024

- I am gearing up to sell another SF property and redeploy those proceeds in 2024. That one will follow a similar approach to last year's. I will not have as much depreciation to offset taxes on this sale as they are sunsetting the accelerated depreciation we can take in year one to 60%. Currently, Congress is working to pass legislation to reinstate 100% accelerated depreciation for RE investors; fingers crossed!

- I am keeping a 4/1 SF house and will attract a Section 8 tenant (wish me luck!) to boost the cash flow to over $1k a month after all utilities, PM, and mortgage costs. I have had mixed results with Section 8 tenants in the past and am leaning on the PM to make this a success.

## 2024 Goals

- Get my property fixed up and sold to reinvest the proceeds.

- Stabilize the Section 8 rental.

- Help other investors utilize the Property Llama software to gain clarity on their portfolio's current performance.

- Help other investors who would benefit from getting involved in passive investing to get involved.

- Raise capital for our projects and create win-win-win scenarios for all parties involved.

# Miller McSwain

My wife and I moved to Colorado Springs in 2022. By day, I am a Nuclear Rocket Scientist, and she is a Biochemist. While these are fantastic jobs that we are thankful for, we have found it much more exciting and fruitful to forge our own path. So, by night (or after work hours), we are real estate investors, pushing our boundaries, acquiring properties, and creating our own financial future.

Our journey into real estate began with purchasing our first property in 2022, a leap of faith that would set the tone for our future endeavors. We bought the property sight unseen, relying on our research, intuition, and faith in our real estate agent. It was a bold move, using our own cash that we saved during college, but it laid the foundation for what would become a series of strategic acquisitions.

In 2023, we continued our momentum by acquiring our second property, once again utilizing our own funds. At this point, we had poured heavily into developing our acquisitions and management systems, so we decided to begin scaling. We expanded our approach by bringing in capital partners for our third and fourth properties. This strategic shift allowed us to scale more rapidly, leveraging the financial backing of passive investors. I took on an active role, with responsibilities such as finding deals, analyzing investments, overseeing remodels, managing tenants, and handling the bookkeeping.

## Strategy

Our initial strategy revolved around house hacking one property per year, a solid starting point that allowed us to gain valuable skills and develop systems from "on the job training". However, as we honed our expertise, we realized the potential to accelerate our growth. We then transitioned to investing in non-owner occupied properties with capital partners and discovered an incredible win-win scenario. Our partners, often having accumulated equity pre-2022, seek to redeploy their capital into more assets as they have previously. However, in this market, finding profitable properties has become quite the challenge since housing values and interest rates have increased drastically. By combining their capital and our expertise, we all share in exceptional cash flow and appreciation from our investments, requiring zero active participation on the capital partners' part.

## How to Achieve Cash Flow in Colorado: Co-Living

Navigating the Colorado market posed challenges, particularly in achieving cash flow through traditional long-term rentals. Our partners experienced this as they attempted to deploy capital themselves using the strategies they've been familiar with. Initially, we also failed to find cash flowing properties in Colorado, until we set our sights on the Co-Living (Rent-by-Room) strategy. In a nutshell, this strategy typically involves renting a single family house to multiple tenants, instead of to one family. This approach has proved to be a game-changer, offering benefits like reduced legal complications compared to short-term rentals, year-round demand, and remarkable vacancy absorption.

Our commitment to providing a premium experience for our residents resembles the Airbnb model. Furnishing shared spaces, supplying essential supplies, regular shared space cleaning, and inclusive utilities contribute to creating a housing experience that surpasses traditional long-term rentals. This approach benefits us as property owners and enriches our residents' lives, addressing the need for affordable housing in the community.

## 2023 Achievements and Progress

As we progressed through 2023, our focus involved systematizing our business. As we focused on scaling, documenting processes for property management and transforming them into efficient systems became paramount. Adding a virtual assistant to oversee these systems allowed us to streamline operations, marking a significant step towards a more hands-off approach. Simultaneously, we ramped up our acquisitions, surpassing our initial goal of house hacking one property per year.

In the realm of personal growth, I prioritized my marriage by implementing intentional practices. Weekly dates, daily compliments, and reading relationship books became pillars of my commitment to creating a solid marital bond. Fitness was an initial focus of mine, although admittedly, I struggled to keep the commitments I set for myself. However, with my wife setting a fitness goal alongside me in 2024, I anticipate a more successful and sustained commitment this year!

## 2024 Annual Goals

Looking ahead to 2024, our ambitions have reached new heights. The overarching goal is to enable the retirement of both my wife and myself from our W-2 jobs. This involves expanding our acquisitions to a new market to meet the demand from our capital partners. We will raise an additional $1.2 million to purchase 8 Co-Living properties in our local market and beyond. Our target is to reach at least $150,000 per year in expected cash flow from our rental portfolio after splitting profits with our partners.

Personally, I have a significant focus on my marriage this year. My goal is to meet my wife's needs 80% of the time, the true goal of a scientist! Every day, I track the state of our relationship, ensuring I am in tune with her and that our personal lives flourish alongside our professional endeavors.

## Bio

Miller McSwain is a Nuclear Rocket Scientist and Co-Living investor. He invests with capital partners, bringing incredible cash flow and appreciation to their portfolios. You can find links to featured podcasts, connect with him, and learn more about his story at www.NotRocket.Co.

# Mitch Conrad

## Gardens Care Senior Living

**The Riches are in the Niches.** As I reflect on our real estate journey, one concept that has propelled our success comes to my mind: the riches are in the niches. Our real estate journey began in 1998 when my son was born, and my wife, Jennifer, chose to stop working to stay home with our kids. That was my impetus, to take action and invest in our first real estate property, a triplex in Aurora. We started with fix-and-hold multifamily properties and then dabbled with a few flips, short-term renting, and some out-of-state properties. While we were reasonably successful with each of these strategies, our real success came when we pivoted after my father-in-law needed care. We began to focus on building a senior living business. Initially, we would accept almost any good deal we could find. We thought the easiest way to start would be to convert a single-family home into a group home for seniors. However, after a few of these home conversions and acquisitions of already operating businesses, we learned that acquiring existing businesses was much easier and faster since all the difficult startup hurdles were already completed. Using our experience from renovating properties was a massive advantage for us in acquiring businesses needing renovation. Each time we renovated a property, we got better at it, and now we are one of the best. Instead of being average or even good at several real estate niches, when we concentrated on senior living and drilled down even further, we became experts at rehabbing buildings and improving operations.

Over the years, this has created what I consider to be an 'unfair advantage' over our competition. It takes time, effort, and continuous learning, but now that we have established ourselves in this niche, we have many advantages. Because of our experience and our investment team, we are usually the best buyer for sellers because they know we are proven closers. Because of our experience and our care team systems, we are usually the best choice for residents and their families because they see the quality of our service. I'm not saying we have all the answers and never make mistakes; we are continually learning, improving, and evolving. We also still have a rental portfolio, a short-term rental, and a landscaping company to maintain our properties, but our core is senior living. The more time, effort, and education put into a niche, the more dominant you will become. We are to a point now where we turn down more deals than we accept. So, I don't think everyone should necessarily start their own senior living company. I believe you should pick a real estate niche, learn, adjust, and pivot as you grow, and become an expert in your niche as you build your 'unfair advantage' over your competition.

Some may argue that diversification is more important than drilling down a niche. I feel that diversification is a defense strategy that has a place in investing, but when you're in growth mode, diversification should be secondary. There are many ways you can diversify your real estate portfolio, even within your niche, investing in different geographic areas, different property sizes, or property classes from class A to class D. For additional diversification, you can diversify outside your niche but still within real estate by choosing another asset class such as single-family, multifamily, industrial, office, short-term rentals, assisted living, sober living, storage, mobile-home parks, etc. We plan to continue working on our 'unfair advantage' in senior living and slowly add to our rental portfolio. At some point down the road, we will probably start investing in more passive asset classes unless our kids want to take the reins and continue growing the senior living business.

I've also had some people ask me when enough is enough. The assets we control are now valued at over $60 million. While it's true that we could stop growing and slide right into retirement, that's not what brings joy and purpose to our lives. We want to impact the way the industry cares for seniors positively. As we continue to raise the bar, other companies will also be forced to improve the care they provide in order to compete with us. We also find joy in creating solid jobs for people in our community. As long as seniors need care, people need employment, and we have the energy and desire for our work, we will continue investing in senior living.

# Gardens Care Portfolio and Project Updates

**Portfolio Numbers.**  We now have 23 Gardens Care locations with 26 buildings and 414 units for seniors (24 independent living apartments, 189 assisted living beds, and 201 memory care beds).  Four small properties are in various stages of renovation and licensing and will open in the first half of 2024.  We currently have 210 employees and 8 contractors who assist with maintenance and renovation projects.

**Renovation Projects.**  In 2022, we acquired eleven assisted living homes from a failing company.  We began renovating the six homes with some residents and then worked on the five vacant properties.  We are required to hold state licenses for each location, and for the six occupied locations, we applied for change-of-ownership licenses, which isn't as challenging as starting a new license.  The state regularly adds more regulations and property requirements, and for a change-of-ownership license, we are grandfathered in for most new property requirements.  The main downside of using a change-of-ownership license is that the previous operator's regulatory compliance history travels with the license and, therefore, remains as part of our history.

Licensing the five vacant properties is a larger project.  When starting a brand new license, we must comply with all new regulations.  Four of the five vacant properties were complete renovations, so we first opened the houses that needed the least amount of work.  However, two homes required an additional full bathroom somewhere in the home.  We developed a plan with an architect that tears out two current full baths, two storage closets, and part of a laundry room to make space for three new full bathrooms in that area.  Of course, this also requires permits and inspections by the fire and state health departments.  We hoped to have all five projects completed in 2023, but we couldn't make that happen.  One house has been opened, two renovations are complete and awaiting final inspections, and the two remaining homes with the bathroom projects are in progress.

**Saddle Rock.** At the end of 2023, we added another community in Aurora to our portfolio. It is a memory care property that is licensed for 64 beds. The property is only eight years old and is in very good shape, which makes it different from most of our other acquisitions. The biggest component of the business plan is getting the expenses under control as the previous management company wasn't profitable, precipitating a sale by the owners. We are also considering adding four more bedrooms to the building, which would increase revenue.

**Company Systems and Efficiencies.** Throughout 2023, we worked on our systems and processes to make our business more efficient and profitable. Below are several of our accomplishments.

- Our internal care communication, reporting, and accountability systems have been greatly improved.

- We changed our workers' compensation insurance carrier for more cost savings.

- We started a 401k program for our employees as an extra incentive for employment with Gardens Care.

- I protested property taxes on many of our properties. That was successful in reducing taxes on almost half of those submissions.

- In the fall of 2023, we decided to hire a business coach to help us reach the next level in efficiency and profitability, so hopefully, I will have some additional progress to report for 2024.

**Employee Retention Credits.** In 2023, we received a sizable refund for 2020 and 2021 through the ERC - Employee Retention Credit Program. We qualified because of the impact and extra expenses Covid placed on our business. The credit amount was based on payroll, and it helped us recover much of the additional staffing and supply expenses we incurred during the pandemic. However, we must now amend our 2020 and 2021 taxes by reducing our payroll expenses by the ERC amounts we received. The net effect is that our income for those years increased by the same amount as the ERC funds, which then increased the taxes for those years. So even though we received funds to help with the extra expenses, we will end up giving a percentage of it back. In 2024, I will work to lessen that tax burden by accelerating the depreciation of more real estate properties.

**Helping Others Start a Senior Living Business.** As a real estate agent, I've been using my experience with clients to help get them started in senior living, and I think we are working on some good options. If you are interested in discussing senior living, don't hesitate to contact me. My advice is to start by acquiring an existing operation to avoid many of the difficult parts of starting from scratch. Such as applying for zoning accommodations, dealing with required community meetings (most neighbors are not supportive), adding fire suppression sprinkler and alarm systems, and complying with physical property regulations such as room square footage, bathroom requirements, grab bars, handrails, ramps, window heights, and sizes, flooring requirements, door widths, and threshold transitions, etc.

**Work-Life Balancing.** I heard someone say that when you're a business owner, there is no such thing as work-life balance, but rather, you're continually working toward balancing the two. I continue to strive to make time for family and friends, health, and traveling. My goal is to move more quality time to the non-work side of the ledger. Last year, I joined a triathlon club, and I've begun training on my weakest segment, which is swimming. So, a triathlon might be in my future for 2024. Jennifer and I took several vacations in 2023, including trips to Grand Cayman, Steamboat, Vail, Costa Rica, Las Vegas, Rome, Alaska, and three trips to our condo in Maui. We also scheduled a family vacation in Maui and plan to make it an annual family event.

# Goals and Direction

**Growth Model.** We have decided that we will no longer add residential assisted living homes to our portfolio. We believe that smaller homes are great for many seniors. Still, it's getting more difficult to scale our resources in so many directions, so as we continue to grow, we will concentrate on larger properties. We are keeping the residential homes we currently have as they are a great compliment to our larger communities, but it would take an incredible residential portfolio to lure us in that direction again.

**Expansion Plans.** We are strongly considering expanding outside Colorado next year, and a 100-bed community has captured our attention, so hopefully, we will have more to report in 2024.

**Development Project.** For the past couple of years, I've written about a development project for building two 16-bed assisted living homes on vacant land adjacent to one of our memory care homes. The land was not sold to us but rather to another developer. This developer was interested in working with us to complete the project we had submitted to the city planning department. However, with the quick rise in interest rates and construction costs, this development team felt the costs were too high for them, so they searched for and found another development team that we are currently negotiating with to determine if this project will continue. More to report next year.

**HUD Loan.** Last year, I reported that in 2024, we planned to move ten senior living homes we financed with a conventional mortgage into a HUD loan. However, in 2025, we can exercise our lease option for a group of eleven properties we acquired in 2022, so we're pushing the HUD loan to 2025 and hopefully placing the 21 residential properties that qualify for HUD into a HUD loan with lower interest rates, a longer term, lower loan-to-values, possible cash-out, and non-recourse.

**App Development.**  We've been working on an app for our business.  We couldn't find an app that does all the employee and family communications and will sync with our electronic medical system.  Our app will also allow families to access and/or receive notifications for medicine passes, meals eaten, and activities in which their family member participates.  We are currently in beta testing.  After completion, we might market it to other senior living providers and daycare centers.

**Employee Housing and Financial Education.**  I would like to expand our housing program for our employees and start a financial education program.  Currently, we are renting some of our apartment units to staff, and I've even given one employee the option to buy the single-family home they are renting.  I'd like to expand these employee benefits, but I haven't found the time or resources yet.

**Franchising.**  We researched franchising and met with some companies that specialize in helping companies franchise their business.  While we think our business and systems would make a good franchise, we've decided that we are going to continue expanding our own portfolio instead.  Franchising would be an entirely new business with lots of legal work, setup costs, and time devoted to preparing to launch such an endeavor.  We continue to have good growth momentum with our own portfolio so we don't want to distract from that at this time.

**Placement Agency.**  We are still considering starting a placement agency to bring additional resident leads to our company; however, as busy as we have been with other projects, we have yet to be able to focus on this startup.

# Bio

Mitch Conrad is a former high school teacher and coach who began his real estate investment career as a side hustle to provide for his family.  After growing a multifamily portfolio in Denver and then expanding out-of-state, he and his wife,

Jennifer, are now focused on senior living.  With 26 buildings across 23 locations in the Denver area, they provide care to 400 seniors and jobs to 200 employees.

## Contact Info

www.GardensCare.com

Mitch@GardensCare.com

303.514.3302

# Nick Elder

Nick Elder is an investor and capital raiser in Denver, CO. After seven years in the Healthcare and Pharmaceutical industry, he transitioned full-time to real estate. Nick is the Co-Founder of Trinity Peak Partners, a firm focused on multifamily acquisitions in Northwest Arkansas and single-family acquisitions in Ohio and Pennsylvania.

## 2023 Reflection

2023, for me, was a year of transformational growth and momentum. New relationships were formed, my career and personal growth took me to the next level, and I accomplished goals I initially thought were out of reach.

I'm walking away from the past year with a new mantra...

Limitations are perceptions.

## 2023 Goals Revisited

Invest $50k as an – *Completed.*

I invested $25k of my Roth IRA in Mamenta as an LP and another $30k in the Samuel Drive Apartments single asset syndication project as an LP. I'm also an investor in National Diversified Funds 5,6 and 7.

My goal is to build a syndication ladder by investing $50k per year over the next 10. I will increase this to $100k per year as my earnings increase and my profits start coming back to me.

Prepare to sell my rental in the first quarter of 2024 and reinvest as an LP or my own investment – *Completed.*

Rather than waiting, I decided to sell my rental property in Q4 2023. It started as a house hack and then turned into a rent-by-the-room rental. I'm holding the profits for liquidity to pursue my own investments.

**Raise $20M**– Not Completed.

I set the bar very high, personally aiming to raise $20M in 2023. I was able to raise more than half. Going into the year, I knew $20M would be an aggressive goal. However, I needed an audacious, maybe unrealistic, goal that would force me to take massive action following a turbulent 2022 when I lost my pharma sales job and pivoted into real estate full-time.

Capitalize $50k into a whole life insurance policy to leverage into other investments – *Not Completed.*

I am reevaluating whether this will be part of my long-term retirement and wealth-building plan. I capitalized $20k. I will likely pursue this strategy only after I've exhausted all other tax-efficient investment and cash storage options.

## 2024 Goals

1. Acquire three value-add apartment projects in Northwest Arkansas.

2. Acquire 20 single-family fix and flips/BRRRR.

3. Raise $20M.

4. Continue building my personal brand through LinkedIn content, podcasts, and speaking arrangements.

## Trinity Peak Partners

I started TPP in 2021 with my partners and longtime friends, Joey and Meredith Schneider. Collectively, we own 35 doors, 29 of which were acquired in the second half of 2023. What started slow three years ago is now gaining momentum and growing steadily as the real estate market and economy soften.

We acquired our first multifamily property in Fayetteville, Arkansas, on December 7 from a distressed seller eager to 1031 into a different project. We negotiated the price to $1.95M (appraised at $2.1M), giving us almost two free units. All tenants were month-to-month, paying an average rent of $640. Market comps on renovated units indicate we will be able to increase the rents to $1,000 - $1,050 and bill back utilities to tenants to increase our Net Operating Income. Our business plan is to relocate all tenants at once, fully renovate the building's exterior and interior units, and lease up at new rents. The status of the economy in 3-5 years will dictate the timing of our exit strategy.

This is a classic value-add strategy we will hone in on, and there are plenty of these available in Northwest Arkansas. The challenge will be sellers coming down to a price that aligns with the market. Those who can source deals that pencil in today's economy will be in a good spot when the market turns in the near future.

## Looking Forward

I'm incredibly excited to see what we accomplish in 2024. I wasn't sure what to expect when we kicked off 2023, but I knew I was in the right place and excited about the future—last year opened my eyes to new possibilities.

The past year wasn't without self-doubt, uncertainty, fear, and stress. Sometimes, I found these emotions to be paralyzing. However, I shifted my mindset to perceive these emotions and thoughts as reasonable and necessary for growth. Everyone who stretches the edges of their comfort zone experiences these emotions. It is a sign of growth. Whether building a business, raising a family, starting a new job, or traveling to a country you've never been before, learn to welcome these thoughts and emotions as a sign that you are moving in the right direction.

Moving forward, I'm leveling up in several ways. I hired a business coach. I joined a referral networking group. I'm buying as much real estate as I possibly can. I'm raising as much money as I possibly can. I'm building my brand and social media presence. I'm surrounding myself with people who will elevate me. And, of course, no year would be complete without a couple of international trips. This year, I'm traveling to Jordan, Oman, Abu Dhabi, and Italy.

I will leave you with a quote currently written on a Post-it note on my computer...

Discipline. Commit. Figure it out later.

Let's Connect!!

Email: nick@irontoncapital.com

Phone: 412-848-7668.

Instagram: @nelderco

LinkedIn – www.linkedin.com/in/nickelderrealestate/

# Paul DeSalvo

My real estate career started shortly after being hired for my dream career in 1999 as a firefighter/paramedic. I quickly realized while sitting around the kitchen table drinking coffee with my fellow brothers and sisters at the firehouse that everyone had some kind of side gig and had to make some extra money. Along with some of the funniest stories and jokes I've ever heard, one of the more interesting topics I really enjoyed was real estate. Many of my brothers and sisters were purchasing their first home after being on the job for a couple of years, and everyone loved hearing about the process. I noticed that when someone would tell their story, it inspired others to believe that they could do it too.

I earned my real estate license in 2002 and started my own company two years later. My wife and I inherited a few properties in 2006 and have been renting them out and updating them over the years. In 2014, my wife and I decided to use some of the equity in a couple of rentals we owned, including our own, to purchase a commercial multifamily apartment building.

We bought our first 11-unit apartment building in 2015. Over the next few years, we continued to buy and sell multiple apartment buildings, two retail centers, and a Natural Grocers.

Currently, we are sitting on some equity and have been thinking about where to go from here. Interest rates have really crushed the market, and we have been frozen on what to do next. So, I started learning more about the local market, reading books, and listening to podcasts. This is where I met Chris Lopez. I was intrigued by what he was doing and what value he was bringing to people interested in real estate investing. I knew I had to meet him and get to know him better. He invited me to be on his podcast and tell the story of what my wife and I had achieved. We also placed our properties into Property Llama and noticed we had a lot of stale equity.

We are now investing in a few syndications. One of these syndications is in Wisconsin, which is a senior living facility with lots of potential and upside. We also recently invested in Vareco and Property Llama. I met with the team several times, and it was a no-brainer to invest with these fantastic people. After listening to Chris's podcast with Red T Homes, I have also met with their team to make a future investment with them.

Below, I will outline what our goals are for 2024. We plan to make some big moves to position ourselves for an opportunity in the commercial Multifamily sector that hasn't been around for many years. We want to be more passive investors and find high-yielding funds that will provide monthly cash flow and a high IRR when sold. We plan to sell our Natural Grocers and invest proceeds into VareCo utilizing a 1031 exchange with a TIC. Initially, I was unaware if we could even go down this route. After researching this option, we can do this. The 1031 with a TIC is becoming more widely used by syndicators and allowed by the IRS if structured properly. Many details need to be vetted by lawyers and CPAs first.

## Goals for 2024:

- Sell Natural Grocers and use a 1031 exchange.

- Meet or exceed the current cash flow from Natural Grocers.

- Rehab a property in the Berkeley area with a large addition, three-car garage, and ADU.

- Sell our townhome in Highlands Ranch and reinvest in a multifamily syndication.

- Explore the sale of several other rentals and invest in funds to make better use of ROE.

- Continue to grow our real estate investing education classes for first responders- **Fire on FIRE**.

- Start a podcast called **"Fire on FIRE,"** Teaching first responders how to invest in real estate.

- Invest in the Property Llama VareCo Fund.

- Invest in Property Llama (the business).

- Explore a cost segregation study.

- Use a self-directed IRA to either loan on or buy SFR.

- Continue to grow cash flow.

- Explore an investment opportunity with a local developer.

# Phillip Austin

Since this is my first time submitting a chapter, I feel obligated to give a short bio and explain how I got into real estate investing.

My background is in hospitality management. I've worked in almost every type of hospitality organization you can imagine, including country clubs, restaurants, corporate events, hotels, music festivals, all of it. In 2019, I took a leap of faith, leaving my dream job, and entered the world of property management. I know what you're thinking, and yes, I am crazy. I worked as a Housekeeping Director at Four Seasons Hotels & Resorts in Denver. I left in the summer of 2019 to join a large national property management company that many of you would recognize. Given my extensive background in operations and customer service, they gave me the opportunity to take over as Director of Operations for their entire market in Colorado, which, at the time, consisted of about 500 doors under management and 10 team members. During my 4 years as Director of Operations, we grew from 500 doors under management to 2,300 doors and roughly 45 team members across the Front Range of Colorado. We also acquired 7 other property management companies, some with under 50 doors and others with over 500 doors. It was hyper-growth and a once-in-a-lifetime opportunity that taught me a lot about real estate investing and how to scale a business, so much so that I chose to leave in 2022 to start my own book of business for property management and purchase our first investment property in Arvada.

As you can imagine, 2023 was an exciting year filled with many unique challenges. Here were my main goals:

## Buy Our First Rental Property – Accomplished

Despite leaving a lucrative salary, starting a business, and getting engaged, my fiancé and I were able to close on our first home in July 2023! We are house hacking a duplex in Arvada, and it's going great so far. After closing in July, we put roughly

$30K into the basement renovations, which included adding a full kitchen and a bathroom renovation, creating a separate entrance for the basement unit, and flipping the laundry room so it's accessible to both the top floor main unit and the basement unit. The monthly rent for the basement is at a modest $1,800/mo and covers roughly 60% of the mortgage. It's not the greatest cash-on-cash return, but hey, at least we got into the market!

## Complete House Hacking Renovations and Lease Basement - Accomplished

This was a daunting project when you purchased your first home at the top of the market and depleted most of your savings. We needed to add a kitchen and create a separate entrance to lease the basement long-term. Those were the two requirements in my book. Short-term was out of the question. As a professional property manager, I know how much work and effort goes into short-term rentals, so I chose smaller margins and smaller headaches. In addition to the basement rehab, we had 1,700 sqft of 80s wallpaper to strip, which I took on myself to save some cash, among many other minor repairs. Sweat equity, baby! All renovations were completed within 30 days, and we were able to lease the basement 45 days after closing. Quick and efficient!

## Start My Brokerage for Property Management – Failed

For the past 4 years, I was the Director of Operations for a large national property management company that many readers would recognize. It was a once-in-a-lifetime opportunity that taught me how to scale a PM company from a few hundred doors to thousands of doors under management. With that said, I've always had the goal of starting my own PM company; however, I was bound by a beefy non-compete/non-solicit agreement, which I was unable to navigate successfully. So, I had to pivot and ended up joining the incredible team at Acorn + Oak in the Spring of 2023 who allowed me to operate my own book of business with minimal constraints and absolute freedom to operate and grow as I see fit. I went from managing thousands of properties and a team of 45 employees to managing 0 properties.

## Onboard 80 Total Doors With New Brokerage – Failed

Since joining Acorn + Oak in May 2023, I've onboarded 59 doors. So, technically, as I write this, I have a few months left to accomplish my goal. Not too shabby! Especially given that we are brand new to the Denver market and have little to no online presence. We are strictly word-of-mouth and referral based. If you need a great property manager who is responsive and actually knows what's going on at your properties, don't hesitate to reach out!

## Get Engaged – Accomplished

This was by far the highlight of my year and one of the greatest days of my life! My fiancé Kristen and I got engaged on August 4, 2023, during a hike from Aspen to Crested Butte. Yes, I know; I did the Classic stereotypical Colorado engagement on a hike, but it couldn't have been any more perfect. If you haven't done the hike over Maroon Bells from Aspen to Crested Butte, I highly recommend it!

The theme of 2024 is save, save, save! We had many significant changes in 2023, including job changes, getting engaged, purchasing our first investment property, moving, and starting a business. Stabilization is critical to position ourselves with enough capital to purchase a 2-4 unit property in 2025. We'll make minor adjustments and improvements to our basement unit while most of the focus goes to growing the business and growing my income so we can build up cash reserves.

## Increase Rent for Basement Unit By 10%

Initially, I listed the 1,700 sqft 2 bed 1 bath basement unit for $2,100 per month. Like many investors with a large rehab, I tried to maximize rent to recover our $30K as quickly as possible. However, since we listed the unit in October, leasing activity was beginning to decrease rapidly, and we had to make significant decreases in rent so we could lease it quickly. After a couple of weeks on the market, we dropped it to $1,800 and had it leased within 2 weeks. If the current tenant decides to move out in June 2024, we'll do a full repaint and carpet replacement throughout and increase the rent to at least $2,000 per month.

## Increase Total Door Count to 150 Doors Under Management

Although I didn't achieve my 2023 goal of 80 doors under management, I'm gaining a lot of momentum going into 2024. We do not have any significant online presence. We do not have a gigantic marketing machine bringing us pay-per-click leads. At Acorn + Oak, we are focused on incremental and referral-based growth. Most of our leads come through word of mouth and referral-based networking, which allows us to pick clients who align best with our values strategically. My goal is to continue cultivating those great relationships I made in 2023 by consistently completing my hustle habits listed below.

### Hustle Habits

- Attend 50 networking events.

- Give 24 referrals -- inside or outside of my network of RE professionals.

- Read 20 books -- non-fiction only.

- More consistent journaling -- does not have to be daily but at least once per week.

- Run 15 miles per week.

### Personal Goals

- Plan our wedding – *all* contracts executed by 12/31/24.

- Run one marathon or triathlon.

- Successfully complete 75 hard – we've tried twice and failed twice.

- Finish paying off student loan debt.

# Shawn Riley

Shawn Riley is an early-stage real estate investor and house hacker who bought his first house hack in 2022 and is passionate about creating freedom for himself and his family through real estate. He is also part of the Keyrenter Property Management team, working in business development and rental analysis.

Connect with him at #620-778-5207

## 2023 Goals, Results, and Lessons Learned

I bought my first investment in January of 2022, a bit of a fixer-upper to house hack it. I spent the first six months of 2022 gutting and remodeling my basement, turning it into a full 2 bed 1 bath apartment with the intention of listing the basement on Airbnb to offset my mortgage. The "Strategy" for many house hackers is to buy 1 deal a year with as little money down as possible, eventually growing a portfolio over a period of 5 years or so. That was my aspiration to be what is called a "Serial House Hacker."

Going into 2023, I had finished my basement remodel and had successfully covered my mortgage. The plan was to finish remodeling my upstairs so I could maximize my income by living in my basement and renting my upstairs unit. Then, once we had enough of a down payment saved, we pushed to purchase the next house hack. By the end of 2023, my goal was to identify and purchase or be under contract for my next house hack!

As each month of 2023 passed, I did not have to pay my mortgage and essentially eliminated my most significant living expense. Although my wife and I had not created financial freedom yet, we realized for the first time in our adult lives we had breathing room and a good amount of it! With higher interest rates, house hacking isn't quite as sexy as it was, and managing two house hacks sounds about twice as hard. So, we decided to hold off on jumping into our next deal, and we are still living in the upstairs of our house hack, even though the downstairs would be more profitable... large widows and sunlight keep us happy!

Instead of trying to grow my portfolio as big as I could as quickly as I could, I decided to enjoy the fruits of my labor. My "rent" was paid, my wife and I are still relatively young, were in good health, and we just wanted to live life and be present. My wife and I are in our mid-twenties, so we have plenty of time to grow our portfolio. Although we still have significant feelings of FOMO regarding real estate investing, we are happy and enjoying each day as it comes, and our upstairs unit is about 75% complete. We could pivot to move downstairs to maximize income during the busy season for short-term rentals.

All in All, if you look at 2023 on paper, we did not move the real estate or financial needle much, but I realized life is not about a certain amount of cash flow or acquiring 10 doors before I am 30. I am passionate about real estate because of the freedom it can provide. I realized we had already created some level of freedom and decided to take a bit of a gap year to enjoy it! This simple yet profound lesson I learned in 2023 is far more valuable to me than even closing on my first house hack in 2022.

## 2024 Goals

**Personal Goal**—My goal for 2024 is to be more present with friends, family, and the community and limit screen time. I want to keep the momentum going from my 2023 lessons learned. I have realized that you must embrace the present while planning for the future.

This would equate to 3-4 camping trips this summer and 10 hikes; I want to go on at least 1 hunting trip and take my beautiful wife on a trip abroad. In December 2023, I deleted Facebook and Instagram on my phone, and I am smart enough to realize I will never need TikTok. For my lifestyle, I just would rather eliminate these distractions.

**Business Goals**: Although this may not be exactly real estate, my wife and I love to camp, so we want to purchase a van camper or camper of some sort. We want to enjoy our hobbies more, but this way, we can rent it out and have it pay for itself. A little bit of rich dad, poor dad strategy for you! It's kind of real estate on wheels, right? If this turns out to be profitable enough, we have thoughts of scaling the business; I like the idea, as the barrier to entry is less than that of real estate.

**Personal Finance Goal**: My wife and I are committing to tracking our personal budget for each month of 2024. We have a savings goal of 40% of our net income. In 2023, we had a similar goal and did great for about three months. If we can keep our budget and savings goal, we should have enough seed money for a real estate investment in 2025-2026.

**Health Goal:** I would like to commit to working out consistently for the next 12 months. In years past, I have worked out for 2-3 months and then taken a 2-3 month break, and of course, I have yet to see the long-term results I desired. Along with working out consistently, I want to nail my nutrition with a high-protein diet to build muscle and slim down a bit. I want to lose 20 lbs. and gain more muscle along the way.

Consistency is my word of the Year for 2024. For each goal I look at, there was a season or time where I did great, but the person I want to be needs to hit these goals consistently. I am a perfectionist, and I need to realize that you don't need perfection daily but consistency over a long period. I have always struggled with New Year's resolutions or big, lofty goals; they seem hard to implement over a long period of time. My goals this Year are more attainable, and I took the time to visualize how I can implement these into my daily life. I want to make these goals a part of my identity. If I consistently hit these goals, I will be a better person and live a richer and more fulfilling life!

# Stephen Lepke

Stephen Lepke is a Denver native, born and raised in the beautiful state of Colorado. He holds a Bachelor's and a master's in science in Mechanical Engineering from the University of Colorado at Boulder and a Master of Business Administration from the Leeds School of Business. He has been a product management technology executive for the past 15 years, a real estate investor for the past 10 years, and a licensed real estate broker for the past five years.

He is a proponent of Gary Keller's Millionaire Real Estate Investor strategies and coaches his clients to implement similar techniques. Stephen maximizes his clients' return based on their risk tolerance through long-term rental, mid-term rental, short-term rental, and value-add real estate investment strategies. Stephen guides other clients along their journey, leveraging his own real estate investment experience to build wealth and financial freedom through real estate.

Connect with Stephen at (303)-570-1729, Stephen@LepkeGroup.com or https://stephenlepke.yourcastle.com/.

## About My Strategy

To learn about my real estate strategy, I feel you must first understand my background and how I landed in my current journey. I grew up in Lakewood, CO, a suburb west of Denver, from the late 80s onwards. The first house I grew up in was at the end of a sleepy cul-de-sac with horses roaming around in the field behind our house. Fifteen years later, my future high school would be built in that field and be filled with over a thousand students. When I was ten, we moved to the South Green Mountain area to a little subdivision on what seemed to be the western edge of the Denver Metro area before entering the mountains. I could hear and see Bandimere Speedway from my bedroom window as dragsters raced up and down the track. Like the last house, we were surrounded by fields with no other developments near ours. Fast forward another ten years, and that field was developed to be the

Solterra development filled with now $1M+ valued homes. So, I have seen Denver grow from being a small cowboy town to the mid-size metroplex that it is today, and I am intimately familiar with the neighborhoods and the real estate.

During the 2008-2010 period, I was finishing my engineering schooling at the University of Colorado at Boulder when the Great Recession hit. I remember vividly working at an internship and thinking that the events unfolding would drastically affect me for years to come. While most of my friends and family's homes were okay, I had some friends who lost their homes and were deeply impacted by the recession. At that point, I saw the messiness of the housing market, the foreclosures, and the bankruptcies as a stark warning that real estate was a risky place to invest, and at any moment, the market could collapse, and so would my family's stability. Therefore, I decided to stay away from the real estate market.

Between the time of 2010 and 2014, not only did I feel risk aversion to real estate due to the Great Recession, but as a Millennial, I wanted the freedom to move and travel as I saw fit. I was early in my career and had no idea of where I would land long term (i.e. location in Denver, a different city, etc.), and so I felt purchasing a home would tie me down to a specific area and restrict my options of movement for at least 5-10 years. As I understood it, once you bought a house, you were stuck with that decision, and it would take at least five years to "get your money back" ... no thanks, this was way too limiting.

However, in 2014, I met some very savvy Real Estate Agents teaching people about wealth building through real estate. I was curious and attended a handful of events and dove into learning more about "house hacking" to live rent free. Up until this point, I had yet to learn that you could purchase a house and then rent out the other rooms in your house to help offset your mortgage. Before, my mental mindset was fixed; however, after these discussions, I shifted into a growth mindset. Furthermore, I learned that not only was buying a house a good investment, but it also did not lock you into a given location for the next 5-10 years. Part of the model

I later learned about was to move every few years and rent out my current residence. I would then put down a small down payment to purchase the next property, increasing my leverage but also increasing my return on equity (ROE) and internal rate of return (IRR).

So, in 2015, I bought my first primary residence, rented out two other rooms, and paid only $400/month net for my mortgage. In 2016, I got married, and we moved to our next house while renting out our first house. In 2018, we moved again and rented out the second house. We have gone through this process enough times now to where we have built reasonable wealth through real estate in under a decade. I picked up my real estate license in 2019 and have been a professional real estate broker/agent since then, helping others leverage my experience for their journey.

## The Millionaire Real Estate Investor

This real estate acquisition model closely follows Gary Keller's Real Estate Millionaire strategy. In that strategy, he has four concepts: 1) Think a Million, 2) Buy a Million, 3) Own a Million, and 4) Receive a Million.

1. In "Think a Million," Gary emphasizes the importance of developing a millionaire mindset. To be successful, one must continually learn, network, and find mentors who can guide and inspire investors.

2. In "Buy a Million," Gary dives into the specifics of identifying investment opportunities and conducting thorough due diligence. There are a lot of ways to find good deals. His book provides insights into finding undervalued properties, negotiating deals, and securing financing. This part of the journey also includes having a solid real estate team, including real estate agents, attorneys, and lenders.

3. In "Own a Million," Gary talks about the challenges and rewards of property ownership. Some of the key success areas in this stage include effective property management, maximizing cash flow, and building equity. At a certain

point, you grow and explore additional strategies for scaling one's real estate portfolio and even diversifying your portfolio within this asset class. These areas (some listed outside the book) include leveraging partnerships, real estate syndications, passive investing, investing in different property types, and diversifying geographically. At this point in your real estate journey, you have accomplished much and are miles ahead of where you started, even though you simply took the next small step at the proper time when building your portfolio.

4. In "Receive a Million," Gary centers around generating passive income and achieving financial freedom. While it may take a lot of time to build up to $1M in passive income through Real Estate, there are ways to systematize your workflows in "Own a Million" to allow investors to step back from day-to-day operations while still earning significant profits. Some additional investment strategies at the most sophisticated levels include rental properties (small scale or commercial size), real estate investment trusts (REITs), and syndications.

Outside of investing using the Millionaire Real Estate model, I have also built real estate investment groups using the BRRRR (Buy, Renovate, Refinance, Rent, Repeat) model to fix and rent other properties in the Denver area. On average, we achieved a Cash on Cash return of 16% and an after-tax IRR of 33%.

I've achieved the "**Own a Million**" threshold and am working on the "**Receive a Million**" milestone. It's been an incredible journey, and I am continually learning and growing in my real estate practices. I'll speak about it further down, but my sophistication in investing has grown dramatically, especially over the past four years, as I continue to find new ways to build wealth through real estate.

# BRRRR Financial Analysis Example

I've always found it helpful to share with people how I underwrite an investment. It allows them to see my transparent process, follow the logic, and see how we mitigate risk when we model an investment properly.

The property below shows the finances behind the first property our investment group bought in Thornton. The house was in terrible shape when we bought it. Even though we purchased it at a bargain price of $180k (4 bed, 2 bath) in 2016, the property had some potential foundation issues, a dog had continuously urinated in one of the rooms, and the basement was unfinished. My partners and I spent the next three months completely reflooring the entire upstairs (removing the original hardwood and laying down luxury vinyl flooring), remodeling the kitchen (new appliances, countertops, created a bar), building a third bedroom upstairs, remodeling the upstairs bathroom, finishing the basement to add two more bedrooms, and refinishing the downstairs bathroom. Given this was our first flip, we did not have a lot of money and performed all of this work on a shoestring budget (~$20k initially) and a lot of sweat equity.

However, the numbers panned out in the end, and we cash-flowed the property very well for the entirety that we held it. Two years later, we refinanced the property and purchased another, performing an even larger remodel on the next property. We sold the first property in 2021, in the middle of the pandemic, for $450k.

The key when making our investments was to ensure we bought the property at a compelling basis (i.e./ purchase price) and that we were within 25% (ideally smaller than that) of our remodel budget. After that, it was essential to execute effectively and place strong tenants who would pay on time and would respect the property. We were fortunate to have great tenants during this time.

Our results spoke for themselves. With our initial investment and after our remodel, our property had a cap rate of 12% (the expected return of the property), a cash-on-cash return of 17% (cash income earned compared with cash invested), and an internal rate of return (IRR) of 47% for the project (5 years). Needless to say, this investment outperformed many other asset classes multiple times over.

If you have questions about the calculations or the spreadsheet, feel free to reach out to me and I can walk you through the analysis. I use many different spreadsheet and analysis tools. The one below was based on a template from the Certified Commercial Investment Member (CCIM) Institute and modified by me to improve some modeling aspects.

Investment Analysis for 5 bed/ 2 bath Single Family in Thornton (Purchase 2016, Sold 2021)

## Annual Property Operating Data

| Property Name | 5 bed 2 bath SFR Thornton, CO | | | | | | | | | |
|---|---|---|---|---|---|---|---|---|---|---|
| Type of Property | 1 | | Purchase Price | | 180,000 | | | | | |
| Size of Property | 1 (Sq. Ft./Units) | | Plus Acquisition Costs | | 35,360 | | | | Rennovation | |
| | | | Plus Loan Fees/Costs | | 1,980 | | | | | |
| Purpose of analysis | Buy side analysis, Fix, and Rent | | Less Mortgages | | 144,000 | | | | | |
| | | | Equals Initial Investment | | 73,340 | | | | | |

| Assessed/Appraised Values | | | | | | | | | | |
|---|---|---|---|---|---|---|---|---|---|---|
| Land | 36,000 | 20% | | | | | | | | |
| Improvements | 144,000 | 80% | | | | | | Amort | Loan | |
| Personal Property | 0 | 0% | | Balance | Periodic Pmt | Pmts/Yr | Interest | Period | Term | |
| Total | 180,000 | 100% | 1st | $144,000 | $708 | 12 | 4.25% | 30 | 30 | |
| | | | 2nd | | | 12 | 4.75% | 30 | 30 | |
| Adjusted Basis as of: | | $215,360 | | $144,000 | | | | | | |

| | $/SQ FT or $/Unit | % of GOI | | | COMMENTS/FOOTNOTES | | | |
|---|---|---|---|---|---|---|---|---|
| ALL FIGURES ARE ANNUAL | | | | | | | | |
| 1 POTENTIAL RENTAL INCOME | | | 27,000 | Median = 2250 / mo | | | | |
| 2 Less: Vacancy & Cr. Losses | ( 2 % of PRI ) | | 540 | | | | | |
| 3 EFFECTIVE RENTAL INCOME | | | 26,460 | | | | | |
| OPERATING EXPENSES: | | | | | | | | |
| 7 Real Estate Taxes | | 2,000 | | Est | | | | |
| 9 Property Insurance | | 1,500 | | Est | | | | |
| 10 Off Site Management | | | | | | | | |
| 14 Repairs and Maintenance | | 2,000 | | Estimated 5% | | | | |
| Utilities + Internet | | | | All else | | | | |
| 29 TOTAL OPERATING EXPENSES | | 20.8% | 5,500 | | | | | |
| 30 NET OPERATING INCOME | | 11.6% | 20,960 | Cap Rate = NOI / purchase price | | Cap Rate | 12% |
| 31 Less: Annual Debt Service | | 247% | 8,501 | DCR Debt Cover Ratio = NOI / annual mortgage | | DCR | 2.47 |
| 35 CASH FLOW BEFORE TAXES | | 17.0% | $12,459 | Cash on $ return = pretax cash flow / down payment | | Cash on Cash | 17% |

Authored by Gary G. Tharp, CCIM   Copyright© 2004 by the CCIM Institute

|  | End of Year: | 5 |
|---|---|---|
| Principal Balance - 1st Mortgage | | 136,397 |
| Principal Balance - 2nd Mortgage | | |
| TOTAL UNPAID BALANCE | | $136,397 |

| PROJECTED SALES PRICE | $447,898 |
|---|---|
| | NA |

CALCULATION OF SALES PROCEEDS AFTER TAX:

| | | |
|---|---|---|
| 17 | Sale Price | 447,898 |
| 18 | -Cost of Sale | 17,916 |
| 19 | -Participation Payment on Sale | |
| 20 | -Mortgage Balance(s) | 130,763 |
| 21 | +Balance of Funded Reserves | |
| 22 | =Sale Proceeds Before Tax | 299,219 |
| 23 | -Tax (Savings): Ordinary Income at 40% of Line 16 | (480) |
| 24 | -Tax: Straight Line Recapture at 25% of Line 11 | 5,429 |
| 25 | -Tax on Capital Gains at 21% of Line 13 | 45,071 |
| 26 | =SALE PROCEEDS AFTER TAX | $249,199 |

**IRR Calculation**

| Year | Cash Flow |
|---|---|
| | (73,340) |
| 1 | 7,731 |
| 2* | 83,433 |
| 3 | 6,880 |
| 4 | 7,270 |
| 5 | 181,798 |
| IRR= | 47% |

*75k Cashout Refi for next investment

# 2023 Lessons Learned

The biggest lesson I learned this year is never to stop learning and to grow continually. I made significant strides this year in learning some of the latest techniques in real estate investing that are helping investors thrive during a time of high interest rates and low deal volume. For one, I learned about passive investing through private equity real estate funds as a Limited Partner. These funds allow you to take a hands off approach to investing, while still being exposed to real estate and leveraging some very capable General Partners in other companies working on some massive projects. The overall return of these funds is between 14%-20% IRR, which is pretty incredible given that the stock market's average return is roughly 8%. While the passive funds don't have as great of a return as the BRRRR mentioned above, they are also a lot less work and still give you great exposure. Through this PE fund, I also learned how to efficiently convert my 401k into a Roth

IRA and minimize my conversion costs using some standard accounting rules that are particularly advantageous to a Limited Partner in real estate investing. Through our existing investment and these funds, we are laying the groundwork of financial independence in the next ten years.

A second VERY important lesson I learned is to ensure the right team of professionals surrounds you. You want to work with top notch people who are not only experts in their field, but also look out for your best interest. Especially in the real estate industry, a lot of shady stuff can go on. Therefore, it is imperative that you work with an agent, lender, attorney, property manager, etc, who knows their stuff and works with integrity to help you meet your goals. In this industry, I feel like everyone can be a mentee or a mentor or both to those who are further along the path. These people are instrumental for you to learn how to adapt and be successful in an ever changing market. It's important to pick the right people who want your success and that everyone's incentives are aligned (ie/ everyone wins).

## 2023 Goals & Results

I am a big goal setter. Every New Year my wife and I sit down and set goals for the year. We think of the big picture goals (where do we want to be in a year, three years, five years, ten years) in addition to the daily habits goals that are required to achieve these longer term visions.

For my real estate business, my 2023 goals were more ambitious than I thought, but relatively speaking, I am making good forward progress in my journey. As our pediatrician says, with respect to our kids, it is not necessarily the exact metric, but the trend, that is important.

1. Find three key RE mentors - Mostly Accomplished.

    a. I found two very solid informal RE mentors who have helped me grow tremendously in my RE profession.

2. Connect with my sphere with one in-person meeting a week - **Mostly Accomplished**.

   a. I connected with a prospective client at least once every other week and have made many more calls to prospective clients to catch up and provide value for their real estate needs.

   b. I have also built some automated tools to help provide newsletters, real estate updates, and other content for my clients. I'd love to build more into the new year.

3. Expand my sophistication of RE investing to include 1) Short-term Term Rentals, 2) Passive Investing, and 3) Dabble in Commercial Investing - **Accomplished**.

   a. I ran my own mountain short-term rental for this past year and learned a lot about the market. While not a slam dunk, the learning experience has been very beneficial for me and my clients. I also invested passively with a local PE fund and look forward to more passive investing in 2024. I am also learning more about commercial real estate (primarily multi-family) and am learning a lot now to position myself well for acquiring a deal or two in 2024-2025 when there are more distressed assets available on the market.

4. Serve ten clients - **Somewhat Accomplished**. I served three clients this year and while I was happy with working with those clients, I want to further improve my communication and the value I provide to my sphere to serve 10+ clients in 2024.

## 2024 Goals

1. Create Three Compelling Real Estate Investing Content Videos.

   a. The best way to become a thought leader in a space is to provide valuable content that exposes people to your thought process. I'd like to build at least three real estate videos that share my knowledge with the broader community and help clients understand the many paths to be successful investing in real estate.

2. Grow My Sphere by 20% and Continue to Provide Valuable Educational Content.

    a. With a few hundred people in my sphere and network, I'd like to grow new meaningful relationships with others whom I meet throughout the year.

    b. I will continue providing free rental reports, portfolio analysis, and home price valuations for my clients to help them make the best investment decision possible.

    c. Join a team accountability group to ensure I am meeting my outreach goals.

    d. If the volume grows to warrant it, I also plan to hire additional people to join my team to increase my capacity (ie. transaction coordinator and marketing coordinator).

3. Help Seven Clients Start the Path to Become Millionaire Real Estate Investors

    a. I want to serve seven different families in their desire to start down the path of becoming Millionaire Real Estate Investors, either through the proscribed model or by helping clients buy their first investment property.

4. Help Five Clients Find New Primary Residences.

    a. I very much enjoy helping friends and family purchase their next primary residence. I find a lot of joy in helping people I care very much about find their next home and lend my professional expertise in their house-hunting journey.

5. Learn More About Passive Investing and Commercial Real Estate (Primarily Multi-Family) and Position an Asset for a 1031 Exchange Upgrade in 2025.

    a. There is a lot of friction in the commercial real estate system at the moment due to high interest rates. I'd like to position some of our investment money to take advantage of a good deal if/when some of the commercial real estate properties become distressed in 2024/2025 (probably picking up a small apartment complex).

b. If there are no solid commercial assets ready to purchase, I'd like to continue my passive investing journey in addition to active investing.

## Conclusion

Investing in real estate is not a silver bullet or a magic wand to building wealth. It takes concerted time and attention to really grow your portfolio. At the same time, with discipline, vision, and a good team, I'm convinced most people can become real estate millionaires if they simply start down the path and keep persevering. Today's current market is particularly tough for buyers and those trying to enter the market for the first time. However, there are also plenty of tricks that you can implement to be successful.

I hope you enjoyed my story, and I wish you the best of luck in your real estate investing career. Please don't hesitate to reach out if I can help you further.

Connect with Stephen at (303)-570-1729, Stephen@LepkeGroup.com or https://stephenlepke.yourcastle.com/.

# Toby Hanson

I remember it like it was yesterday. I'd just left the title company after closing my first house! I was excited, but little did I know my mood was about to change.

With keys in hand, I called my buddy to tell him the good news and to start packing. I'd shown him the place a few weeks back, and he'd said he was down to move in with his wife and son if I bought it. It was a 4 bed/3 bath 3,300 sq ft model home with a pool table, a built-in bar in the basement, and a hot tub on the back deck.

I had just moved back to Colorado from Florida and had some money saved from my job at FedEx. I'd decided to buy the biggest house I could and do a "house hack," renting out the other rooms to my friend and his family to help cover my mortgage.

What led up to this decision started with my friend Marcy. She told me how her equity gain from her house in Naples, Florida, the previous year was almost as much as her annual income. Another Friend owned a duplex. He not only lived there for free because he could live on one side and rent out the other, but he also made $200 a month over the mortgage.

My thinking at the time was to ride the equity up for a few years, then sell that house and buy two smaller houses, live in one, and rent the other. Then, I would save up to buy another home every few years and rent the one I'd been living in. The goal was to own a portfolio of 5 rentals, pay them off one at a time, and retire on the rental income.

But that's not what happened...

My friend responded to my "good news" by saying, "Dude, I never expected you to qualify for that house; we can't afford to live there." I went from excited to feeling like I just got punched in the gut! If he couldn't afford half the rent, how did he expect me to cover it all on my own?  I was working two jobs, one of which was commission-based, and my income fluctuated.

My 'house hacking' plan seemed to crumble before it began, but the house was mine, so I started scrambling to find roommates.  It worked out for a while, but I made a rushed decision and took the first two roommates who applied.

The second guy didn't get along with the first one and moved out after the first month.  Then, the first guy started coming up with excuses as to why he couldn't pay the rent.  I kicked him out, and a coworker moved in with his girlfriend.  That lasted for about six months, but my income as a loan officer started to fall off a cliff due to the global financial meltdown going on at the time.

Long story short, I lost the house to foreclosure a year later.  I couldn't sell it for what I owed and didn't know about subject-to or short sales then.  Looking back, it could have been a deal for someone, and I could have avoided foreclosure.

With my credit in the dumps and my tail between my legs, I returned to renting and working in restaurants to make ends meet.  But every fall is a chance to rise again.  I refused to let this setback define my story.  Armed with lessons from the past and a relentless spirit, I dove back into the world of real estate, this time with a new ally.

I had been studying digital marketing and decided to focus on paid Facebook and Google ads to find motivated sellers so I could buy properties at a discount.  I also started going to real estate meetups to learn from experts and expand my network. I ended up at a group called "Badass Real Estate Investors," where I met James Brown, who also has a chapter in this book.

After a few meetings, we determined our goals aligned and joined forces.  We shared a vision and a commitment to break free from the unpredictable tides of traditional investments.  We knew we would not get where we wanted to be in the timeframe we'd set for ourselves solely through stocks, bonds, and mutual funds.

I thought I was doing everything right, following society's plan, yet my retirement goals kept getting farther away. I decided I would have to earn more, save more, or find better investments if I had any chance of retiring before I was 80 years old.

Many people find themselves stuck in a similar situation. They're battling volatile markets and low returns and are tired of the unpredictability and insecurity of traditional investments. They don't want to "ride it out" anymore and want to get off the roller coaster. They're worried about not having enough to maintain their lifestyle after retirement and don't want to end up working until they die.

So, we set out to find a safe, secure way to get above-average returns. We looked at the many ways to invest in real estate. We did not want to create a job for ourselves, so flipping was out, and we wanted to avoid the hassles of being a landlord, like dealing with tenants, trash, and toilets.

We liked the ability to generate monthly cash flow, appreciation, and the tax benefits of the buy-and-hold method, but we knew it would take decades to build up the cash flow needed to retire comfortably. We also wanted the big paydays that flipping houses could provide.

We knew there had to be a better way and could see so much opportunity in this space; we just weren't capitalizing on it. We were determined to figure out a better way to invest.

## Introducing Hybrid REI

So, after far more entrepreneurial scars than we'd like to admit, including investing over $100k into education, coaching, and high-end masterminds, we eventually cracked the code on a method that maximizes profits with minimal risk, and it's a win-win for all.

With the guidance of some amazing mentors, we have refined an innovative approach that gives us and our investor partners a higher return on investment with more protection than traditional methods that rely on speculation, taking on the risks of large rehab projects, or dealing with nightmare tenants.

We got creative by combining the benefits of fix-and-flip and buy-and-hold into a single strategy and calling it Hybrid Real Estate Investing. With Hybrid, we get the benefits of each strategy while eliminating the drawbacks of both.

This new strategy allows us to profit big on nice houses in nice neighborhoods that require little to no work. It eliminates the risk that comes with significant rehabs and dealing with unreliable or unethical contractors.

Hybrid REI is a "reverse lease option." We start with a pre-vetted buyer who currently cannot qualify for a mortgage. They are good people with a sizeable down payment and good income, but they may be self-employed and claim too much in tax deductions, which is smart unless you need to show the bank how much you actually make. Other situations include doctors and lawyers with a high debt-to-income ratio due to student loans or someone who is late on a payment because they got sick or hurt.

We, or our investor partner, buy the house the resident-buyer picked out and sell it to them using a pre-negotiated lease option. The lease option buyer is responsible for most of the maintenance and repairs, so virtually all the cash flow goes to our bottom line.

Unlike typical renters, our residents have an owner's mindset. They have "skin-in-the-game" in the form of a 5-figure non-refundable option fee collected upfront, so we know they are serious about buying and will take great care of the property. When we have a high-quality resident with pride of ownership, we get passive income every month without the usual landlord headaches and large backend profits when they exercise their option to purchase, which usually happens in 1-3 years.

We also do "property-first" lease options. With these, we give the buyer 10 years to exercise their option to purchase and set the price where we estimate the value to be in about five years. We've honed our marketing to find great deals in strong markets at a discount or with a low fixed-rate mortgage we can take over so it cash flows in this high-interest environment. We stay involved as owner-managers, so our capital partners don't have to deal with tenant or property-related issues. Since our goals are aligned, we are motivated to keep costs down and profits up.

We realized we had a "Blue Ocean Strategy." After years of focusing on our strategy, it's been paying off. Real estate agents, lenders, and other people in the industry now come to us as the experts in lease options. James even teaches real estate agents and lenders a continuing education class about the right way to do rent-to-own, so everyone wins.

We love that we can help deserving families become homeowners while also helping our investor partners invest passively in real estate so they can free up time, get monthly cash flow and tax benefits, and retire in comfort. Their fear of outliving their savings or being unable to afford the lifestyle they want for retirement is now replaced with a proven strategy. Our approach curbs the risk of traditional market volatility and gives our investor partners a plan for growth and predictability.

Hybrid REI was born from the trials of our past and the lessons it taught us. This strategy isn't just another investment method; it is our testament to resilience, creativity, and the relentless pursuit of financial freedom. It is our path to a safer, more innovative future of prosperity. We're not just building portfolios but legacies, one property at a time.

# Launching A Private Investor Club

People heard we had access to capital through our investor base and started pitching us their deals. We saw many opportunities and asked ourselves how we could take advantage of these more significant deals and pool money between us and our investors. We weren't experts in all asset classes we looked at, such as multifamily, mobile home parks, self-storage, and short-term rentals. However, James was a Blue Spruce Multifamily Mastermind member and had a solid foundation for how syndications work.

We wanted a way to participate in these opportunities without diminishing what we were already doing. A while back, I remembered a conversation I had with an investment banker. He described how his ultra-high-net-worth clients were getting high returns with very low risk.

He explained how risk is pushed down to the public market and how the best investments were typically reserved for institutional investors and often had $1,000,000 minimums. He then told me how we could access these types of investments through a Private Investor Club or a Feeder Fund, and that's when I knew I was on to something.

I started researching and found a mastermind. We joined and learned all about Fund of Funds. His mastermind gave us access to top-tier investments and the people and resources to set up our Fund. We launched the Accelerated Capital Alliance, an investor club for busy professionals who want to invest in alternative assets like commercial real estate.

Now, we invite others to invest alongside us in the best opportunities so they can get high returns without high risk. We find outstanding managers who specialize in one thing and have a long history of making consistent distributions with a business plan executed multiple times. We pool capital inside our investor club to get better terms by writing one large check to our investment opportunities.

With everything happening worldwide, this is the perfect time to diversify away from the stock market and the standard 60/40 portfolio and get into safe, secure alternative investments with a high upside. Of course, risk is involved in these investments, but they can be mitigated through comprehensive due diligence on the operator and the opportunity.

## Better Returns with Less Risk

By linking up with other investor clubs, we've increased our leverage with operators, allowing us to negotiate even better terms for us and our members. We also reduced the risk of getting into a bad deal by adding a third layer of due diligence divided among the different fund managers by each of their strengths.

Most of the time, someone in our collective brings us the deal and knows the operator personally. Naturally, we start by doing a background check and verifying their track record. Next, we have someone who lives near the project who can be our 'boots on the ground' and another who loves diving into the private placement memorandum (PPM).

If everything checks out, we'll have a few people underwrite the deal to ensure the numbers match the operator's numbers. This is a comprehensive process, and by dividing up the responsibilities, we can evaluate deals quickly and with less stress. This enables us to move fast without being rushed, which is another competitive advantage.

We wanted to help both accredited and non-accredited investors, so in addition to some great Reg D 506c opportunities, we also seek out 506b deals that will allow for up to 35 non-accredited investors. Since we can't advertise 506b deals and need a pre-existing relationship with investors, we get on a Capital Acceleration Call to review their current investment allocation and investing goals. Then, we create an 'Investor Roadmap' to achieve their goals.

For us, this isn't just about opening doors; it's about creating new ones. From the meticulous vetting of deals to offering a lifeline to both accredited and non-accredited investors, our mission is clear. We want to redefine the investment landscape and democratize the power of capital. By strategically reducing risk and volatility while enhancing returns, we're not just changing portfolios; we're changing lives. We are cutting down decades of work, saving and redefining the very concept of retirement and financial freedom.

Today, our journey continues as we seek new alliances, connecting with fellow investors who share our vision and values. It's more than investments; it's about crafting a legacy of prosperity and security, about finding the perfect synergy between investors and opportunities.

## Why I Do What I Do

I believe everyone should control their financial destiny. I think most of us reading this book would agree that real estate is a powerful wealth-generating vehicle. And if you don't, you should put this one down.

I also believe that each of us has dreams and ideas we would love to share with the world and that becoming financially free is the first step. Once we have the freedom of time, we don't have to worry about making money to survive; we can begin to focus on what truly drives us. I believe that becoming wealthy is the key to making a real impact because it provides the resources to turn our aspirations into reality.

Because of these beliefs, I strive to help others achieve financial freedom along with me and create real wealth through real estate investing so we can make the world better in our own unique way. The Colorado Cash-Flow Club is just one way I'm doing this.

The CCFC is a free monthly meetup where we teach attendees how to get started in real estate investing. It's a combination of networking and education where we help facilitate getting deals done.  Other groups want to charge thousands or even tens of thousands of dollars to get started in REI.  I believe people should use that money to invest directly in real estate, and we're here to help them do that.

I suggest writing down exactly why you want financial freedom so it's crystal clear.  Then, put it somewhere where you can't help but see it every day.  The most surefire way of achieving your dreams is by keeping them in the forefront of your mind and pursuing them relentlessly.  If you want to come to our meetup, go to ColoradoCashFlowClub.com.  You will be able to network in our online portal and get notified of our live events.

## 2023 Lessons Learned

We are constantly bombarded with different ways to make money in real estate, and it's challenging to stay focused.  I realize I need to say 'no' to more.  I can't do it all, and I need to surround myself with intelligent, driven, successful people who can help build our business.

I've also been spending too much time on low-value tasks and content.  The saying "Garbage in, garbage out" rings true.  I haven't been watching cat videos (meow), but I've spent too much time on YouTube listening to economic forecasts and "crash bros' predicting another 2008.  I agree that a type of 2008 is already happening in the commercial real estate sector.  Mostly in office and multifamily, but that is also where the opportunities are if you know what you are doing.

## 2024 Goals

- Focus.

- Be a giver.

- 10X my income.

- Level-up my network.

- Read and study 12 books.

- Grow the Investor Club to 500 members.

- Raise $10M for awesome projects while generating safe, secure, double-digit returns!

To 10X in 2024, I need to raise my floor. I must raise my standards on what I spend my time on and what I say 'yes' to.

I'm committing to eliminating 80% of the low-value tasks and content I consume. YouTube is primarily repetitive and webinars have some content but are not actionable and are designed to sell something.

I'm going to focus on 80% paid content, including audiobooks and courses. I'm starting with a 50/50 ratio of creating/consuming content, with the goal of 80% creating and 20% consuming. I've been consuming 80% content and creating 20%. So, more creating, less consuming, and primarily only consuming high-value paid content.

Creating more high-value content like blog and social media posts, books, newsletters, training, videos, and podcasts, along with some social outreach and in-person relationship building, will lead to more calls with investors, which leads to more capital raised.

In addition to dropping 80% of low-value tasks, I need to focus on Who rather than how. Who can I add to the team? Who can I delegate the essential activities to?

# Vikas Agarwal

This is the first time I am contributing to this book, so let me start by sharing my background as a professional and an investor.

I live in Denver with my wife and our two sons (5 and 2). We moved to Denver in August 2023 after 8 years in Minneapolis, MN. Before that, I lived in South Dakota, Iowa, Florida, Ohio, and Illinois. Let's start by talking about my background as a professional and how I got to this point.

I came to the US in 2003 as a student in the full-time MBA program at the University of Illinois, Urbana-Champaign. I gained my first Master's in India in Computer Applications and worked for a tech start-up for more than 2 years before flying to the US for my MBA. After college, I worked for many global companies with growing responsibilities. After the financial crash of 2008, my interest in real estate grew, and I started studying the residential and commercial real estate market. As they say, taking the first step is the most challenging part of any journey; it took me many years to muster enough courage to acquire my first investment property, a single-family home, in 2012 in Tampa, FL. Since then, I have not looked back. I continued to acquire single-family properties in Florida until 2018 when I moved to Minnesota with my wife, and we started acquiring properties in Minnesota. Our next big inflection point came in 2020 when we acquired our first commercial real estate, a Family Dollar. With COVID-19 raging worldwide, I thought Dollar Stores would become indispensable to a big part of the US population's everyday needs.

In the last four years, we have continued to build our commercial property portfolio, and now we have eight properties in Minnesota, Wisconsin, Illinois (Chicago MSA), New Mexico, and Tennessee. My last three properties were all medical properties with long-term leases.

# Investment Strategy

Post Covid, the Fed's monetary policy has created significant headwinds for the real estate world. Take a look at the Fed interest rate in the last 10 years (Actual interest rate is solid) and the projected (dasshed) for the next 3 years. We are enduring the highest interest rates in the last more than 10 years and the projections show us that rates will only come down gradually and will settle at around 2.5% by the end of 2026.

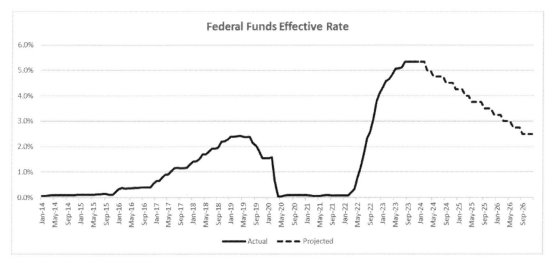

Source: Source: Board of Governors of the Federal Reserve System (US) and Federal Reserve, Summary of Economic Projections, December 13, 2023.

What does this mean for investors like you and me? The questions most of us are dealing with are: Will it make sense to acquire money now, given that money is so expensive? Higher interest rates mean the cost of debt is high, which in turn means you must have higher returns (cap rate) to make sense of acquisitions. This becomes tricky when the cap rates have not increased in the same proportion as the interest rate. That has been my observation for the last 4-5 years, starting from a couple of years before COVID-19, during COVID-19 when Fed rates were practically zero, and COVID-19 when interest rates were historically high. When money is cheap to borrow, there are too many buyers in the market, and many investors are willing to throw an unjustified amount of money at any investment-worthy property; in other words, the Cap rate is too low.  Since money was cheap to borrow, we saw an artificial boom in the economy that restricted the supply of good quality stable properties in the market.  I remember looking for quality properties daily but not finding them due to limited supply.  If anything came up in the market, there would be too much competition with other buyers, essentially making it a sellers' market.

In the current environment, even though money is expensive to borrow, many more quality properties are coming to the market (I will share my definition of good quality properties in a bit), and there is little competition among the buyers.  I believe buyers are in "wait and watch" mode right now and want interest rates to come down significantly from the current level before they think about acquiring again.  This creates a unique opportunity for investors willing to take a longer-term view.  Invest now in high-quality properties and wait for interest rates to come down in a few years before refinancing.  Now, you have higher returns on high-quality properties.  So, this is what I would consider a high-quality property,

1. Properties where the tenant's industry is internet-resistant and stable in economic cycles.  My focus is on medical properties.

2. Properties with around at least 12 to 15 years of absolute NNN lease.

3. A relatively newly built property no more than 5-10 years of age.

4. Strong demographics in the 3-mile radius.

5. Corporate Guaranteed lease agreement and strong financials of the parent company.

## 2023 Goals

My goals for 2023 were twofold,

1. Stabilize the properties I acquired in the previous three years: I acquired 7 commercial properties from 2020 to 2022, some of which were gross

leased. I needed to develop a work-life balance so I could devote enough time during the day to manage the properties and take care of everyday issues. This was partially achieved. I have close to 100% occupancy with maintenance contracts in place (for gross lease properties). Developing a work-life balance is evolving in the right direction, but I think this will require more decisions to be made on my end in 2024 to ensure I am not stealing time from my family/kids to manage the portfolio.

2. Continue to acquire high-quality properties: I did not acquire any new property in 2023. There are a couple of reasons for that

    a. High-interest rate but no compensatory uptick in cap rates: This also formed the basis for my investment strategy for 2024 to 2026, which I narrated earlier. Right now, interest rates are high, but high-quality properties are also on the market, so let's take advantage of this situation and refinance in a couple of years when interest rates go to a more reasonable level.

    b. Keeping my powder dry: My general philosophy about investment is, no deal is better than a bad deal. I am ok if I miss one or two good deals if I am not sure about them, whereas I end up with one or two not-so-good properties when I'm not sure about them. I came close to acquiring a couple of commercial properties in 2023 and had executed an LOI (Letter of Intent) as well, but during the due diligence, I estimated that the risk level was higher than what I was comfortable with, given my investment philosophy and what I promise to my investors. So, it's better to sit tight with equity and prepare for new opportunities in 2024.

## 2024 Goals

My goals for 2024 are an extension of my 2023 goals.

1. Continue to strike the right work-life balance: This was partially achieved in 2023, and I need to continue to work on it. I am contemplating hiring part-time help for property management and some other administrative work.

2. Continue to acquire high-quality properties: From my 2023 experience, I now have clarity in my thoughts/strategy to ride out this high-interest rate environment with confidence. This goal is not just for 2024 but also for many years to come.

3. Create a platform to offer investment opportunities to other interested investors: I believe my investment strategy can deliver high returns with low risk. The benchmark behind my investment strategy is Investment Grade Corporate Bonds (rated BAA by Moody's or BBB by S&P and Fitch). The goal is to invest in commercial properties where the risk is lower than or at least on par with these Corp bonds, BUT returns are higher than what these bonds typically deliver. I plan to raise equity from accredited investors for these high-quality properties.

## Connect with Vikas Agarwal

I am always interested in growing my network and meeting new people. We get better in our trade by meeting and learning from others. I would love to hear from you, share our thoughts and strategies, and learn from each other. The best way to reach me is as follows,

Email: Vikas@arkacapitalholdings.com

Website: www.ArkaCapitalHoldings.com

# Book Sponsors

Thank you to our book sponsors. Our sponsors possess expertise in their respective fields. As you're building your team, please consider utilizing their services.

Disclosure: Our recommended experts are paid sponsors for this book. I have financial interests in Envision Advisors, Property Llama, Property Llama Capital, and Curtis St Media.

NOVA NMLS 3087 / EQUAL HOUSING OPPORTUNITY

# Troy Howell - NOVA Home Loans - NMLS 311477

- Services: Correspondent lending. Very flexible lending products for residential real estate investing. High level support and communication.

- Connect: [troyhowell.novahomeloans.com](troyhowell.novahomeloans.com), (303) 520-6603

## What Does NOVA Home Loans Do?

For over 40 years, we've been focused on helping homeowners find the perfect loan to fit their financial needs and personal goals. Working with NOVA is a personalized experience from initial application to final loan closing and beyond. We will be with you every step of the way toward successful homeownership. Nova prides itself on efficiency and a commitment to professionalism, thriving to provide the best customer experience possible. To better manage expectations, we process all loan applications in-house from start to finish. We also allow you to apply for a home loan directly on our website via a digital application powered by Ellie Mae. This makes it easy to fill out a loan application from any device, securely upload documents, link financial accounts, eSign documents, and more. Once approved you can track loan progress, receive updates, and contact your loan team if you have questions. Start working with NOVA & Troy Howell today!

# Investment Community of the Rockies - ICOR

- Services: Real Estate Investors Association (REIA) serving Denver Metro, Colorado Springs, Fort Collins, and Northern Colorado as well as real estate and rental property investors across the state.

- Connect: Troy Miller, Troy@icorockies.com , Call (970) 682-4267

## What Does ICOR Do?

ICOR is a Real Estate Investors Association (or REIA) founded in 2007 and is currently owned and led by Troy Miller. His philosophy about Real Estate Investing is founded on the belief that we all become better Investors by helping each other, that "the rising tide lifts all boats," which interestingly enough is where ICOR's annual membership award receives its name. Those who not only are excelling in real estate personally but contribute by supporting those in the community around them.

ICOR is more than just a Meetup. We provide credible, valuable investing information and a community of serious investors to help you meet your goals!

ICOR is Colorado's only nationally recognized & award-winning real estate investors association (REIA) serving Denver Metro, Colorado Springs, Fort Collins & Northern Colorado as well as real estate & rental property investors across the state.

## Keyrenter Property Management

- Services: Helps you build a successful rental investment portfolio by handling the day-to-day challenges of managing property.

- Connect: Brandon Scholten, brandon@keyrenterdenver.com
  Call (720) 735-7497

## What Does Key Renter Do?

Keyrenter Property Management Denver provides rental solutions for homeowners and real estate investors in the metro area who are interested in transforming their properties into passive income. It offers various services, from property marketing and thorough applicant screening to tenant placement and 24/7 maintenance services. Keyrenter's team of experts can take the clients' burden of managing their rental off their hands so they can get back to what matters to them.

QUALIFIED INTERMEDIARY

## Tax Deferred Exchanges – 1031X

- **Services**: Nationwide tax deferred 1031 exchanges. Personalized strategies at a single, low, flat rate. 30 years and more than $3.5 billion safely deferred.

- **Connect**: www.1031x.com, exchange@1031x.com, Call (888) 899-1031

## What Does 1031X Do?

1031X offers a one-on-one personalized 1031 exchange process. We help investors protect equity and save tax dollars through tax-deferred exchanges. When investors or business owners sell appreciated real estate, the tax authorities often take 25-35%. We help put a stop to that. We have experience working in every state, with every property category, and building every exchange structure. At 1031X, you'll find the nation's most innovative and client-obsessed 1031 intermediary. This means a fully digital, service-heavy, and secure 1031 process no matter where you are.

# Equity Trust

- Services: Self-Directed IRAs and 1031 Exchanges

- Connect: Adam Sypniewski, adam@midlandtrust.com, Call (312) 767-6863

## What Does Equity Trust Do?

Equity Trust Company and its predecessor companies have been privately owned by the Desich family since 1974. We invite you to reimagine your retirement by enabling you to invest your IRA or other account into alternative assets such as real estate, private equity, precious metals, cryptocurrency, and more.

Equity Trust empowers individual investors and financial professionals by removing the barriers to investment freedom.

Equity Trust's track record of service excellence, paired with streamlined technology, is unmatched in the industry.

At Equity Trust, you can create a customized portfolio and investment strategy in your tax-advantaged account. See why Investopedia named us the Best Self-Directed IRA Company.

# Investor Friendly Agents – Envision Advisors

- Services: Colorado investor-friendly realtors who build, grow, and optimize their clients' real estate portfolios through buying and selling investment properties.

- Connect: www.DenverInvestmentRealEstate.com, Call 303-548-0846 Info@EnvisionREA.com

## What Does Envision Advisors Do?

Envision Advisors focuses on investors who want to house hack or buy rental properties that are small multifamily properties, duplexes and single-family rentals. Whether the investor is new or has a large portfolio—Envision Advisors can help clients figure out and execute a strategy.

Our agents want to help clients build long-term wealth through real estate. We don't do short term projects like fix and flips, but instead help people who want to accumulate wealth over the next 15 to 20 years.

# Optimize Your Rental Portfolio – Property Llama

- Services: Property Llama lets you track and benchmark your investments' performance, as well as find ways to optimize your portfolio for better returns.

- Connect: www.PropetyLlama.com

## What Does Property Llama Do?

The only app you'll ever need to manage your real estate portfolio. Property Llama gives you detailed insight into portfolio performance and helps you optimize for faster returns in four steps:

1. Upload Your Properties and Define Your Goals

2. Benchmark and Track Asset Performance

3. Model Different "What If" Scenarios

4. Uncover Hidden Opportunities to Accelerate Returns

## Passive Investing for Active Landlords – Property Llama Capital

- Services: Property Llama Capital specializes in putting together passive real estate investing deals across multiple market

- Connect: https://capital.PropetyLlama.com

### What Does Property Llama Capital Do?

Passive real estate investing allows you to build wealth without the hands-on responsibilities of being a landlord. Property Llama Capital specializes in putting together passive real estate investing deals across multiple markets. Passive investors can diversify their portfolios and mitigate risk by participating in these curated opportunities. With passive investing through Property Llama Capital, you can earn returns from real estate while pursuing other professional and personal pursuits.

# Your Dream Career

Most people I've hired have come from the local investment community because they heard about a position through our podcast or email list. We have such a super talented crew, that I want to keep getting more of the "right people on the bus" from our local investment community.

There are two main qualities we look for:

**Talented individuals**—Our philosophy is put people in positions that play to their strengths and interests. It sets the individual up for success and follows our "divide and conquer" strategy for giving clients the best service and experience.

**Cultural fit**—Every organization has its own culture. Culture is a huge factor in success and long-term retention. People who responded from podcasts are already familiar with culture and know it is the right fit for them.

With the recent growth of new companies, I'm always on the lookout for talented individuals to join our team. Visit our careers page for more details and recent job openings at www.DenverInvestmentRealEstate.com/Careers.

Made in United States
Troutdale, OR
09/11/2024

22738973R00108